From Ruth to Lamentations

Poetry and Conversation

Jock Stein

Illustrated by Margaret Stein

British Library Cataloguing in Publication Data:
a catalogue record for this publication
is available from the British Library

ISBN   978-1-912052-60-8

Typeset in 11.5 pt Minion Pro at Haddington, Scotland

Printed by the Book Factory

Notes

This book is written at a popular level, but for those who are familiar with the phrase, the poetry is a form of research through creative practice. It is a brief introduction to seven Old Testament books, but one which allows the poems themselves to comment on those books and how they might relate to life today. It is not a 'commentary' on the books (though there is plenty of 'comment', and references are given to some proper commentaries).

Generally the version of the Bible quoted is the New Revised Standard Version. 'Israel' is the context for the story of Ruth, a Moabite woman who joined the people of Israel (or Israelites), but for the stories from later periods, 'Jews' is the word used by the NRSV for the people taken into exile, and then gradually returning to the land of Israel. *Yehudim* originally meant simply the people of Judah, but within the Old Testament it is the book of Esther which marks it coming to have a religious meaning.[3] I often use 'Jewish people' because it is considered more polite, but 'Jew' when it is unnatural to do otherwise.

Where I can, I use God instead of a deity pronoun, since God has no gender, but where that becomes too fussy grammatically I use the old-fashioned 'he', which Jean Sharpin and I are used to. Readers may imagine alternatives if they wish.

For dates, BCE is before the Common Era, CE is during the Common Era. OT is Old Testament, NT New Testament.

---

3 John Goldingay, *Ezra, Nehemiah and Esther for Everyone*, SPCK, London 2013, 167. Goldingay prefers the cognate name 'Judahites', and occasionally 'the Jewish people'.

Introduction

Jean Sharpin, a retired philosophy and RE teacher, became the 'colleague' who helped me write *From Cosmos to Canaan*, verse, conversation and introduction to the first six books of the Bible, Genesis to Joshua. She must have been a great example for those who argue that agnostics can teach RE well. Anyhow, Jean is still around, so far surviving her struggle with Parkinson's, thanks to good medication, and seems well able to question me and draw out bits of wisdom from both of us on Zoom – that tells you this is written during the lockdown period of 2020, when the world had to find ways to cope with corona virus.

A member of my family, much keener on non-fiction books, was rather shocked to discover that Jean was not actually a living person. Were she that, of course I would not be sharing such intimate details about her life as I do in this book.

You may miss the various Edinburgh places of refreshment we met in before, but you will not miss Jean's sharp mind and East Coast sense of humour. (Do you know the difference between East and West Coast wit, at least in central Scotland? In the West the jokes are in your face, in the East you nod politely, and then fall about three days later.)

Good poetry, like the Scriptures, should be accessible to everyone, East or West – but, as with the Scriptures, a bit of explanation can help, which is why these books are a mixture of verse and commentary. As William Carlos Williams once said,[4] "You should never explain a poem – but it always helps". Again, I have used different poetic forms; these, once the norm in poetry, have become much less common during my lifetime, but I would

---

4 During a talk at Harvard University in 1951.

not be surprised if the balance between form and freedom swings back towards form.

The Hebrew Bible is divided into three sections:

Torah (Law)　　　　　– Genesis to Deuteronomy

Nevi'im (Prophets)　– Joshua, Judges, Samuel, Kings,
　　　　　　　　　　　Isaiah, Jeremiah, Ezekiel, 12 'minor' Prophets

Ketuvim (Writings)　– Psalms, Proverbs, Job, Song of Songs,
　　　　　　　　　　　Ruth, Lamentations, Ecclesiastes, Esther,
　　　　　　　　　　　Daniel, Ezra, Nehemiah, Chronicles

This book omits the Psalms; Proverbs and Job are known as 'the poetical books' and the next five as the *megillot* or 'scrolls', making seven for this book. They are all very different, but we will follow the order in the English Bible, shown on the Contents page, which puts two women first.

The artwork in the book is by my wife Margaret. She has kindly and skilfully illustrated at least two other books I have been involved with – *Ephesus to Laodicea*, by Clifford and Monica Hill, and my own Memoir, *Jock's Journey.*

Below the quill pen on the cover is a drop of blood, which reminds us that all seven books featured in *From Ruth to Lamentations* are concerned with our common humanity, even if in Ruth there is a special concern with the bloodline of King David, and in Esther the story of an attempted pogrom against Jewish blood. Job has had to endure the death of his children, and the loss of health and reputation. As he endures the criticism and false counsel of his friends, he see himself as innocent as the murdered Abel,[5] and cries out, "O earth, do not cover my blood".

In the story of Israel and its characters, we can discover ourselves, if we wish, even if we have to go to another book, Isaiah, to see how all that is part of a bigger picture, where God says of his servant Israel, "I will give you as a light to the nations".[6]

---

5 John Goldingay, *Job for Everyone*, SPCK, London 2013, 89, commenting on Job 16:18.

6 Isaiah 49:6.

Contents

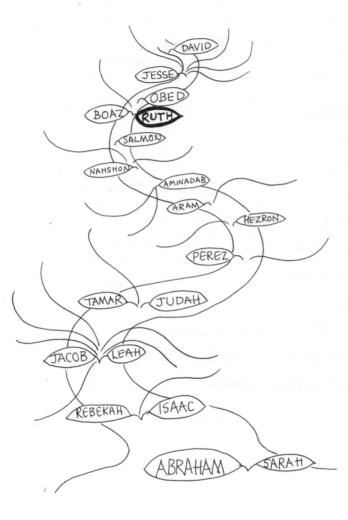

"She bore a son . . . they named him Obed; he became
the father of Jesse, the father of David." Ruth 4:13,17

Chapter 1   Ruth

"It was a big relief to me when I first read Ruth," said Jean. "I realised the Bible was not so racist after all."

"Not *so* racist – you mean that books like Ruth are there to sweeten the pill?"

"Well, the main message of the Old Testament seems to be that God was on the side of the Israelites, and that a Jewish leader – call him Messiah – will one day come and take over the world."

I had to agree with Jean, even if both Jewish and Christian people hold that Messiah's rule will be the best thing the world has ever known. The final chapter of the OT doesn't say that in so many words, it just says that when the day of the Lord comes, the righteous will tread down the wicked, the faithful should remember the teaching of Moses, and that parents and children will be reconciled.

I was tempted to tell Jean not to separate fact and value, and say that the OT hints, and the NT spells out that God chose the Jews for the sake of the world. But that would be throwing philosophy in her face, and anyhow I had a suspicion Jean was winding me up – not so easy to pick up these things on Zoom. Instead I quoted the old rhyme:

How odd of God to choose the Jews!
Yet not so odd as those who choose
a Jewish God, and spurn the Jews.

"Jean," I continued, "it seems to me that most Jews and Christians have taken this whole thing pragmatically. We expect God to bring in his kingdom, but in the meantime we need to get on with living faithfully, and that of course includes not being racist. I've already written two poems on Ruth. One is a simple ballad, outlining the story, and linking it to the New Testament."

By this time I had mastered screen share, so it was easy to show Jean poems.

Love in Violent Times

Love unveiled in violent times,
call it war and peace:
tragedy and climate change,
tension and release

all lie behind this narrative
of Naomi and Ruth,
their travels and their choices,
their faith, their hope, their truth.

One Israelite, two Moabites,
three widowed and bereft;
the old one took one daughter-in-law
back home to Israel, left

the other with her people; Ruth
clung on to Naomi
and to her trust in God, who gave
her new identity.

In Bethlehem at harvest time
Ruth caught a farmer's eye,
the rest, they say, is history
– or providence – that's why

Ruth features in the family tree
of Jesus, mentioned there
with Tamar, Rahab, Bathsheba,
(though Matthew took good care

to call the last 'Uriah's wife').
These four have pride of place
in such a man's world, showing us
a Saviour of mixed race.

"Cunning," said Jean, "taking a shot at racism and sexism in the same poem."

I decided to take it as a compliment. "Did you follow the reference to Matthew?" I asked.

"Of course." (Not much gets past Jean.) "Uriah was like Ruth, not an Israelite, so presumably Matthew wanted to stress what you spell out in the poem, that Jesus was of mixed race, and therefore the gospel is not just for Jews."

Perhaps that wasn't so much a compliment – good poems are supposed to leave things for the reader to work out . . . but then what about all the readers who actually want a few things spelled out, so they can understand a poem better? Sometimes you can't win.

Immediately before Ruth in the OT, the book of Judges gives us a series of snapshots of different Israelite tribes trying to get established in a land with enemies all around. A pattern is repeated, falling away from God, invasion and hardship, calling on God and finding a leader who rescues them – for a while. By the end of that book, readers are left to shake their heads over what is going on within the tribes themselves, with a final word of wisdom, "In those days there was no king in Israel; all the people did what was right in their own eyes."

The rest of the OT establishes that even when there was a king in Israel, things could go badly wrong, but after the nasty stories which close the book of Judges, Ruth comes like a breath of fresh air, a simple story of goodness triumphing over disaster, and a key link in the line of David, whose own flawed reign became a symbol of Messiah's reign. Most scholars think Ruth was written down as we have it during the reign of David, since the final genealogy stops at David, but it could be later. Jewish tradition regards Samuel as the author.

"Samuel seems a calm sort of man, moving around Israel as a judge, in a violent era," said Jean. "There's a calmness about the book of Ruth, in the middle of awful things going on. Like that poem, 'Love in violent times.'"

"Yes, it's like hearing a refugee from Syria talking quietly about his family life back home, when you know his life has been turned upside down."

Like many good stories, Ruth starts with a series of calamities: famine, exile in the land of Moab, bereavement. Three women all grieving the loss of husbands. That was what took me into the second poem I had already written on the book of Ruth:

Grave Business

Grave business indeed,
deciding one's place of resurrection.

For Abraham and Sarah,
diplomatic settlement.

For most of us, like Moses,
not a reference on a map.[5]

For Ruth, a pledge to live
beside her own adopted mother,

receiving care and counsel
up to the last lodge: a promise

God was pleased to honour
in the birth of Obed, truly

son for Naomi,
and resurrection of her line.

"I don't like anachronism," said Jean. "Abraham didn't believe in resurrection, even if my brother came to believe before he died."[6]

Jean was referring to her late brother who had recently died in a Glasgow hospital. I suppose if I had been more caring I would have picked that up and got her to talk about it. But I was a little irritated.

---

5 Deuteronomy 34:6.

6 Interestingly, the New Testament suggests that he did (Hebrews 11:19) – by looking for a meaning hidden in Abraham's words and attitude.

"Listen," I said testily, "poets can make connections without committing all the players to agree with them. 'Place of resurrection' is a beautiful mindset for Christians in the Hebrides thinking about burial, and the place was important enough for Abraham, whatever he did or didn't think about life after death."

I don't mind Jean disagreeing with me, that's how I learn. But there was something in her tone that bothered me. For the moment, I left it. Ruth was enough to be going on with, Ruth and her decision to leave her own people and go back from Moab with her mother-in-law.

"Jean, I agree there is nothing about resurrection in the book of Ruth. Just that wonderful commitment of Ruth to her Naomi. It reads best in the old King James Version:

Intreat me not to leave thee,

or to return from following after thee:

for whither thou goest, I will go;

and where thou lodgest, I will lodge:

thy people shall be my people,

and thy God my God.

Where thou diest, will I die,

and there will I be buried."

Ruth's sister has decided to return to her own land of Moab, so the first chapter ends with the two women, Naomi and Ruth, back in Bethlehem, at the beginning of the barley harvest.

The way the story is told, there are a series of wonderful coincidences – Ruth happens to glean in the field of Naomi's relative Boaz, Boaz happens to notice her, and we have not simply an 'arranged marriage', but a freely chosen (or at least freely cemented) love relationship. Underneath, at least two other things are going on: Naomi is scheming to find her daughter-in-law a new husband, and God is planning to sort things out for Naomi and her posterity.

In Chapter 2, Boaz recognises that Ruth has sought shelter under the wings of the God of Israel. In Chapter 3, Ruth asks him to spread his cloak over her – but the word in Hebrew is the same, meaning something you wrap round for protection, and it can be translated as wings or cloak. So we are invited to hold together God's good purpose, and our own responsibility, in our everyday lives. The other books we look at, especially Job and Lamentations, will admit how difficult this can sometimes be, but Ruth (and Esther) call us to think in this positive way. Neither of them took life's hardships lying down.

Lying Down

When Chilion died, hope prostrated.
Ruth lay down upon it, called it grief.
Later, she staggered to her feet,
measured out her options,
laid them at the feet of Naomi.

She lay wherever Naomi laid down
her head, her faith, her life.
Each hour with horizontal play
of feelings under the horizon,
grief and hope in awful lockstep.

How many foreigners lie prostrate
at the feet of someone who might
feed them, love them, use them?
Even underneath the knees
of those who will abuse them?

Sometimes faith and hope work out,
like Boaz taking care of Ruth, and
(rest your worry, trust the story)
showing honour, keeping faith
with law and love and Naomi.

"I don't buy that chaste 'lying at Boaz' feet' all night," said Jean.[7] "Look what Ruth was wearing when she left Naomi that night. Make up, perfume? It's obvious Ruth offered herself to Boaz and he took full advantage of her offer. It's not the first time a lover has been sent away before first light so people don't suspect anything."

I don't often disagree outright with Jean, but this time I let fly. "Jean," I said, "it's easy to read things into an ancient text from our modern perspective. I'm just glad that some societies are not as sex-obsessed as our own one. But even if you are right, Boaz knew that sleeping with someone implied a commitment to make the relationship permanent, unlike the attitude of casual sex today."

There's an important issue behind this. Always, when you read a document from another culture, there will be things that either jar or seem strange. The temptation is to jump to the conclusion that either "something is wrong with the text" (perhaps it has got corrupted) or "something is wrong with the writer" (perhaps he is being less than honest, or maybe it is just spin).[8] An elaborate way to put this is to say that we have moved over the past two centuries, in the West at least, from a hermeneutic of trust, to a hermeneutic of suspicion.[9] With the Bible, my own view is that trust and understanding should move together and feed each other.

Lack of trust: we used to complain about security procedures at airports – now (writing this at the start of lockdown) we wonder

---

7 Hosea 9:1 indicates that prostitutes visited threshing floors, and Exodus 4:5 connects 'feet' with the sexual organs, which is why the issue in the end turns upon the character of Boaz and Ruth as presented in the story.

8 I say "just spin" because of course we all speak from a particular point of view, so there is an element of spin in all communication. But 'spin' can be honest or less than honest. And behind all communication lies the question of what is a proper worldview to hold, and whether two people speaking share the same worldview.

9 Useful academic books dealing with this include Paul Ricoeur, *Essays on Biblical Interpretation*, L. Mudge (ed.), SPCK, London 1981, Anthony Thiselton, *New Horizons in Hermeneutics*, Zondervan, Grand Rapids 1992, Iain Provan, *The Reformation and the Right Reading of Scripture*, Baylor University Press, Waco, TX 2017.

if we will ever go to an airport again. Back in 2012, waiting in Malta Airport, I wrote this:

Air Travel

Travellers and their hand held bits now pass
in pulses through security, essential hourglass,
then settle with relief or something stronger
round the buffet. Departure queues grow longer
at the gates, as up to date procedures level
down the quality of flying. So, what devil
in the legislative detail causes so much checking
in and out? Perhaps we're wired for wrecking
every chance we get to live more simply. Trust
has flown, and now our masters must
just bite these bitter bullets, and accept
the consequence of faith so badly kept.

"Trust is the vital lubricant for society, as it is for families," said Jean. "I could see why Nicola Sturgeon kept asking people to trust her during lockdown – and by and large people did."

"No doubt Nicola and Boris will both be found wanting when assessment is made of decisions made in the early days of the pandemic. Politics is a hard and unpredictable game, and politicians deserve prayer and forgiveness as well as judgment. It's not surprising that the Old Testament wisdom books focus on daily life rather than affairs of state."

I didn't need to explain to Jean that those 'wisdom books'[10] overlapped with the 'Writings' – but Ruth, Esther and Lamentations are not actually counted in that category. In Job you get the question, "But where can wisdom be found?" and I would say there is plenty of it in these three books, not least because they are about the lives of real people.

---

10   Strictly, the 'wisdom books' are Job, some of the Psalms, Proverbs, Ecclesiastes, Song of Songs, and in the 'Apocrypha' the book of Wisdom and Sirach (or Ecclesiasticus).

According to Eugene Peterson in *The Message*, the 'wisdom books' insist that nothing in life can be omitted or slighted if we decide to take God seriously. "The wisdom writers keep us . . . attentive to the entire range of human experiences that God the Spirit uses to fashion a life of holy salvation in each of us." That means from cradle to grave – or in the case of the book of Ruth, from the death of Naomi's husband to the birth of her grandson Obed, who became in turn the grandfather of King David.

When you get to my age, friends die. I learned a lot from one of my spiritual directors, Michael Butler-Burns, and wrote this poem in memory of him:

Uncommon Sense

Uncommon sense. The quest that took him
to the edge, leaving the rest to make
their own accommodations, take
their chosen shallow bows

while Michael let the Spirit slowly,
firmly chip away the rust in practice,
hoover up the dust in doctrine. This
new age where science welds our thought

to modern dogmas of its own,
yet also melds with ancient wisdom,
was a coalface, and a well to drink from,
mixing every drop with faith and hope.

Uncommon sense. The love that took him
slowly by surprise, gave him a language
richer than he knew, has turned a page
and leaves us waiting, lost and found.

Wisdom in the Hebrew tradition is practical wisdom, wisdom that works in practice, not the Greek version which is more intellectual.

One of the lovely things about the book of Ruth is that it is a simple story about the wisdom of trust, trust in God and trust in people. Of course you can be let down, but wisdom is also about knowing which risks to take.

I was sharing this with Jean (she probably thought I was rabbiting on, but Jean always knows when to blunt her sharp comments), and she said politely, "Why don't you save all that for the book of Proverbs, and get back to Ruth?"

Of course she was right. We were still just at the start of the last chapter.

There are lawyers and lawyers. Some are just legalists, doing a job. Others want to see law fulfil its main purposes, which are to protect and guide people, and enable a society to live at peace with the values it has chosen to adopt. Boaz would have made a good advocate; he knew that the law of his times gave priority to one of his kinsmen, but with that priority came certain duties, one of which was to look after Ruth.

"The way Boaz argued his case reminds me just a little of Portia in *The Merchant of Venice*," Jean commented.

"Great play, but the anti-Semitism jars today."

"Which takes us back to where you started – the book of Ruth is a quiet rebellion against racism. If we only had the book of Joshua we'd get the wrong message."

"That's why Marcion[11] wanted to eliminate so much of the Old Testament which he saw as violent, and some might say racist as well."

"And followed by all those who want to tear down statues of people with views of which they don't approve."

"Did you notice that someone even daubed 'Racist King' on Robert the Bruce's statue in Bannockburn?" I said.

---

11 Marcion, son of a bishop according to Hippolytus, was a wealthy ship-owner who went to Rome about 140 C.E. and worked out what he saw as a gospel of love without law, which meant that he rejected the Old Testament, and ended up only accepting ten of Paul's letters and an edited version of Luke.

"I don't suppose it occurred to them that Bruce had Norman and English blood, and married a wife from Ireland."

We shouldn't judge a movement by its lunatic fringe. Black lives do matter, and even if tearing down statues is not the only or even the wisest thing to do, symbolic protest has a place in our own history, as in the removal of statues at the Reformation. It's certainly there in the book of Judges (6:25-27).

In the end Edinburgh Council decided to put a plaque at the foot of Henry Dundas' statue in St Andrew's Square to explain his part in delaying the abolition of slavery bill. (They also recognised it would cost rather a lot to pull it down!) We do well to try and explain our history – just as the narrator of Ruth does in 4:7-8, though that is merely to explain a custom "in former times" of sealing a legal agreement by the first party to the arrangement giving his sandal to the other.[12] It is a witness to the importance of law, whatever Marcion (and others who take Augustine's "love, and do what you like" out of context) may have thought.

And a witness to the importance of family. I thought of the "mothers of Israel", and the extended neighbourhood family who name the grandson whom Naomi will nurse for Ruth.

What's in a Name?

Obed, servant, worshipper,
child of love and law,
restorer of family line,
nourisher of old age:
named by local women,
nursed by Naomi
honoured in lineage.

A name he did not choose,
a nature to be learned,
an attitude uncommon,
a grace so rare and beautiful
described the king himself,
Isaiah's chosen one,
the servant of the Lord.

---

12 For the link between feet and ownership in Israel, see John Hamlin's commentary on Ruth, *Surely There is a Future* (Eerdmans 1996), 58-9; and in Scotland see Neil Oliver, *A History of Scotland* (Weidenfeld & Nicolson 2009), 48-9..

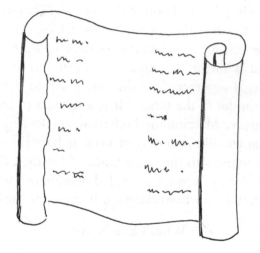

"On that night the king could not sleep, and he gave orders
to bring the book of records, the annals,
and they were read to the king."   Esther 6:1

Chapter 2   Esther

Esther is another book in the 'five scrolls', which were set for liturgical use at five Hebrew festivals. In Hebrew it is Hadassah, usually translated as 'myrtle', but maybe from the Akkadian word for 'bride', which would fit that Biblical metaphor for God's people, and give a reason for including the book in the canon of Scripture.

Who Rules the Rulers?

Kanōn: *a rule, a measuring stick (Greek)*

We call some people petty tyrants,
name them from our safe perspective,
tut-tut North Korea, Belarus.

We like to praise democracy,
which once meant people ruled by laws
inherited from Israel,

but mellowed by the ways of Christ
declared and handed down in books
we call our Bible, canon chosen

for its principles of justice,
set down there to put our rulers
on a moral democratic leash,

guide them how to do their work,
know when to say 'no way' – resign
if standards fail, to keep some faith.

Who rules our rulers, if and when
the canon loses power to fire
its holy words, its measured wisdom?

Esther is used at the Feast of Purim at the end of the year – and whereas the other four were simply attached to a festival because their content related to it, this Purim Festival is celebrated because of the story the book of Esther recounts. The Hebrew word *purim* means 'lots', part of the story as we shall see, but a little strange because one message of the book is that God's providence overrules chance. As Proverbs 16:33 has it,

> The lot is thrown into the lap,
> but the decision is the Lord's alone.

Esther is a story from the time of exile in the Babylonian empire, set between the return recorded in Ezra 1 to rebuild the temple, and the later ventures of Ezra and Nehemiah. Xerxes – the Greek name, Ahasuerus is the Hebrew version – was a chauvinistic king with a wife called Vashti and a big harem. When Vashti objected to being 'shown off' at a drinking party for the royal (male) staff, the king put her away. (Maybe Vashti wanted a way out, anything better than being a royal puppet.) At a beauty contest to select a new queen, Esther – a Jewish orphan brought up by her cousin Mordecai – proves to be the winner. However, the villain of the story, Haman, gets angry because Mordecai will not bow down to him.

Why would Mordecai not bow down to Haman? In Daniel, three faithful Jewish leaders refused to bow down to a statue, but giving people respect, even prostration, is not forbidden in Scripture. One clue in the story is that Haman is named as a descendant of the Amalekites, enemies of Israel. Anyhow, Haman was really annoyed when Mordecai would not bow down to him, and correctly recognised that his behaviour connected with the fact he was a Jew. So he plotted a pogrom of all Jewish people in the empire.

"When I started teaching, Hitler's plan to eliminate the Jewish people was fresh in people's memory," Jean remarked. "That made the book of Esther very topical."

"Not least in Scotland," I said, "with Jane Haining losing her life in Auschwitz."[13]

---

13 Read *Jane Haining – a Life of Love and Courage* by Mary Miller (Birlinn, Edinburgh 2019).

The rest of the book tells how the tables get turned, Haman and his family executed, Mordecai given high office, and the Jews prosper. All without mention of God. Some years ago I wrote a poem about this kind of 'divine providence' in Esther:

The Mills of God

We see them going through the mill,
victims of crime
or maybe just someone's ill will;

how commonly God loses teeth;
time after time
those mills take us beyond belief

into a world where fate just leers
and borrows names
like Xerxes, surfacing the fears

of Jews, who fear that they will die
through vile games
by Haman, foe of Mordecai.

No righteous Miller's mentioned here,
no gumsy God
is slagged for failing to appear,

but Esther's faith and courage show
how all in all
the mills of God grind slow,
but grind exceeding small.

"You would expect God to come into the story somewhere, to get a little of the credit," was what Jean said to me as we talked about the book of Esther.

"That's one of the things I have learned from the book," I commented. "You don't have to keep bringing God artificially into human life, just because it seems the pious thing to do. It works when it is natural – think of Odion Ighalo praising God when he scores a goal – but it can lead to 'pious talk' which ends up hypocritical."

"Human life seems to get on well enough without God. God has never knocked very loudly on my door."

"It seems God is happy to remain anonymous, at least most of the time. C.S. Lewis did say that God whispers to us in our pleasures and shouts to us in our griefs."

"Lewis also admitted that going through his own grief was pretty hard work!" rejoined Jean.

"Yes, it showed him again the attraction of atheism – as if he didn't know it from his early life."

With hindsight, I could have asked if God had ever knocked *quietly* on Jean's door. I have this tendency to stay on an intellectual level, and Jean is enough of a friend that I don't need to do that. But actually she is just the same, so we get on well.

The chemistry of friendship is often strange. Sometimes opposites attract, sometimes opposites repel. I found myself writing a short poem about it, and thinking about the wonderful and mysterious fact that God calls us friends.

Where I Belong

Well travelled, but maybe housebound;
rooted, but with peculiar freedom;
cosmopolitan, but peasant flavoured;
generally, in love with everything
that works and sings and mends:
such is the company of all God's friends.

Back to Esther – a girl who in the story is not at all disadvantaged, in looks or in courage. But living in a world where men were in charge. When the previous queen rebels, Vashti is removed from office because it is feared, if the king allows her behaviour, it will give the green light to all the women in the kingdom to assert themselves as she did. Vashti disappears from the story, an unsung heroine who sets all in motion.

The Disappeared

Vashti, I feel for you, banished to a harem of women
                                    past their prime. You wore a crown
and warmed the highest bed of empire reaching
                        all way round the Indian Ocean.
You pillow talked with power, you ruled
                            your private realm in Babylonia.
You answered to 'first lady', top of the ladder
                        under the glass ceiling.
Did you plan to throw all that away to fate?
Did you try to strike a blow for women everywhere?
Or did you snap when Xerxes lined you up to flaunt your beauty
for his drunken guests? Was he prone to marriage rape,
to borrow future language? Were you desperate?

Vashti, I grieve for you, leading a cascade of women and men
                                    abused by power.
You were disappeared from glory, and from Bible story.
                                Men discussed,
decided on your fate. Your brave outspoken folly was proclaimed
                            in all the media,
tweeted to the ends of empire so that every man might rule
                                his wife and vent his lust
without correction. You were desperate!

Vashti, I'm grateful to you, trying to light a candle, even though
                                a male gale blew it out.
You occupy an opening chapter, others wrote some more
                            and now the fight is bolder,
everywhere. King Xerxes knew you stood for every woman
                                in his empire, and we know
you stand for everyone who feels the hand of power unjustly
                                on their shoulder.
Linda Norgrove, Malala Yousafzai, Jo Cox –
we feel for you, we grieve for you, we're grateful to you.

Jean was quiet after I shared this poem. With Zoom it's hard to read emotions. I began to wonder if I should have emailed the poem instead, and given Jean more time to respond. What I never expected was this: "Jock, you could add my name at the end of that poem. You touched a nerve that is still raw after fifty years."

"Do you want to say more?"

"It was my tutor at university. I'll tell you about it another day."

Jean recovered, and began to give me a hard time for being condescending in that poem, as she saw it. I had been expecting a bit of praise for writing a feminist poem! I had to learn that for a man to write such a poem can be suspect, seen as men still trying to solve problems for women, the old knight errant stuff.

She continued, "Women themselves will deal with this problem. If you want to help, that's fine, but don't think you can fix it for us. Have you heard of Hildegard of Bingen?"

"The medieval poet and saint?"

"She was a lot more than that! She was a polymath, like Leonardo da Vinci: an expert in medicine, music, building and gardening. In her prime she was a counsellor consulted by leaders of Church and State. She led a monastery, though the local clergy did not always like her energy and gifts; with the prejudice of their time, and perhaps out of jealousy, they restricted her title to '*Magistra*', not the more senior 'Abbess'."

As a writer and composer, Hildegard described herself as "a feather on the breath of God". I wrote a poem once about one of her compositions:

Symphonia Virginum, by Hildegard of Bingen

A feather blowing in the wind: it raced
past Forrest Gump, unusual man. Go back
one thousand years, till Hildegard embraced
that feather as a metaphor of life with God,
his breath full filling her in mind and soul
to set her free for Benedict to mark her 'saint'.

Magistra, not abbess; carving out a role
as preacher, poet, counsellor, composer,
writer, project manager; her wisdom praised
across a continent. Her plainsong smiled
at heaven, while she taught and gazed
at God: "O Trinity, you're music and you're life!"

What has this to do with Esther, who is neither the seductive woman we will meet in Proverbs 5, nor the virtuous woman of Proverbs 31? Simply that Hildegard, like Ruth and Esther, is an example of women who become heroines in eras and cultures where it was men who were supposed to be heroes. There is a rabbinic prayer for male Jews from the second century CE which includes the words, "I thank you God, that you have not made me a Gentile, or a woman or a slave. . ." Nowadays, of course, it is understood as simply giving thanks for difference . . . well, I prefer nice spin to nasty.

Actually, that prayer is unexpected, because the Old Testament never says outright that a woman must obey her husband,[14] and there are a number of feisty women like Shiprah and Puah in Exodus, Deborah (and even Samson's mother) in Judges. But Christians likewise by the second and third centuries had picked on one or two texts which seem to denigrate women, and left behind the balance of Scriptural teaching on the mutuality of men and women.

While you can equally make the case that Christian teaching liberated women, you find sexism somewhere in most if not every culture. I began thinking about a proverb I learned from my own mother:

A dog, a woman and a walnut tree
the more you beat them, the better they be.

I also remembered a poem I wrote about it years later, when I was at the Los Olivos retreat centre in the Spanish Sierra Nevada.

---

14 Goldingay 2013, 159.

Almond Harvest in the Sierra Nevada

That scurrilous poem about a walnut tree
– so ignorant of women and dogs –
has been knocked sideways, sieved pure
in the almond harvest
when I saw *señores* beating, beating,
beating branches with long poles,
and a solitary *mujer* gathering,
raking the nuts off black matting,
stacking the almonds
in sacks piled at the foot of a tree
with a sense of achievement,
and a *perro* barking.

We moved on to Chapter 2, three years later in Xerxes' reign, where we meet Esther herself, and her guardian Mordecai. There was already a hint of perfume in the book of Ruth, and in this chapter we get fairly full details of a beauty treatment regime which lasted for a whole year. After that, Xerxes himself did the judging in a very intimate way – and Esther won the contest. She became queen, but of course under the same limitations as Vashti.

It was at this point Jean told me a bit more about what happened. It was during her second year, when she had got to know one of her lecturers, a Dr Playwell. She was sitting beside him when he started touching her.

"At first I just froze, it was completely unexpected. I couldn't even say anything. Then I managed to get up, and leave the room. I thought he'd get the message, but a few weeks later the man actually propositioned me. I was shocked, and decided to go to the Head of Department. The guy (all men in those days) listened, and said he would have a word with Playwell – but not to take it any further, as it would be my word against his. He also warned me that it wouldn't do my career any good if I wanted to pursue academic life."

"Was there any form of counselling in your day?"

"Of course not! But I got over it – that's what we did in those days. The man became distant, and I was glad of that. Except that when it came to the final exams, I'd been unwell and there was some consultation with staff about whether I should get a First. I didn't, and I often wondered why."

Our stories, as we know them, are often full of unfinished business. With Bible stories, the business usually (but not always) does get finished. That's why there is an important postscript to Act 1 of the Esther story – Mordecai, who seems at this point to be a minor civil servant, hears about a plot to assassinate the king, tells Esther, who tells the king, and the coup is thwarted. The details are noted in the royal register.

Act 2 scene 1 introduces Haman, the villain. Five times in the book we are told that he is the grandson of "an Agagite". Agag was the Amalekite king whom Samuel "hewed in pieces before the Lord" in 1 Samuel 15 (not such a calm episode in the life of Samuel) and after the Amalekites attacked Israel on their journey through the wilderness they became long term enemies.

Haman becomes king's favourite, and all the officials are instructed to bow down to him. As we have seen, Haman is furious at Mordecai's refusal, and persuades the king to let him not only deal with Mordecai, but all the Jewish people in the whole empire (with a sweetener for the king's finances). So Haman sends out an edict in the king's name, for a pogrom on a particular date which has been chosen by lot – *pur*, plural *purim* – and the name of the festival is there to remind people that the providence of God is more important than the chance decisions of life.

In scene 2, Mordecai dresses in sackcloth and resigns his post. Esther, who of course is not privy to state business, is informed and has a conversation with Mordecai through intermediaries. It ends with Mordecai challenging the queen to appeal directly to the king. This is more challenging than it might seem, as such an initiative could result in death unless the king "held out the golden sceptre" to agree to hear the appeal.

For Such a Time as This

A chance to win, a chance to die,
a future forced into a flick of time,
a second spun out to eternity.
Who knows if Esther's shocking stab
at Xerxes' chauvinistic sceptre hand
will smash the ceiling, or the glass
prove proof against the bullets
made by Mordecai and fired by her,
so conscious of her frailty?

God rolls a six, God rolls a one.
Who knows how God may stack the dice,
or tell us that the game's a bogey,
Einstein right, and Haman lost to wrong.
This tale is gifted to a line of women,
underlings who seize the day
and call the bluff of overlords
who may stay shadows on their thrones
but find their chancy schemes outdone.

This took us to the centre, if not quite the climax of the story, and
Esther left at the end of Chapter 4 fasting with her people before
putting her life on the line. There had to be a poem for such a time,
and a reference to Einstein's famous comment that "God does not
play dice", which some scientists like, and others say is more about
theology than science.[15]

"It's a long time since theology was 'queen of the sciences,'"
said Jean, "even if your teacher got a prize for that book called
Theological Science."[16]

I am a sucker for these digressions. "Jean, did you know about
Cardinal Newman and the Catholic University of Ireland?"

---

15 Einstein was a lifelong sceptic about quantum physics, which he regarded
as too random, hence the famous quotation.

16 *Theological Science*, by T. F. Torrance, was awarded the Templeton Prize
for Religion in 1978.

For once, I had the advantage of Jean. "Yes, Newman was asked to give a series of lectures in preparation for founding a new university. He argued for a liberal education which would explore relationships between subjects. And he said that without theology,

> the curriculum will disintegrate into a fragmented multiplicity of disciplines, each . . . claiming autonomy in its own sphere. Some will of course draw on each other (as physics does on mathematics), but there will be no conception of a whole to which each discipline contributes a part.[17]

"Jean, there is theology as a servant queen."[18]

It was time to get back to Queen Esther and her mission – life or death not only for her but for her people. At this point, the king was unaware she was a Jew, or related to Mordecai. Well, when Esther appears, she wins the king's favour. He knew she must be wanting something big, and he offers her half his kingdom (a metaphor, of course). Esther simply asks him to bring Haman and join her at a banquet. When they appear, Esther delays her request, and invites them to come back the following night.

This gives a space for two key things to happen, as the narrative builds. Haman erects a high gallows pole to hang Mordecai on, and the king has a sleepless night. Xerxes asks for the record book of his reign to be read to him, and his ears prick up at the story of the recent assassination attempt. "What honour has Mordecai received for this?" he asks. "None."

It it now early morning, and Haman arrives. There follows that famous question, "What shall be done for the man whom the king wishes to honour?" Haman, assuming it refers to himself, advises the king that it requires a celebrity procession through the streets with a herald praising the honoured man. "Good," says the king, "away and fix that for Mordecai, lead him through the streets yourself."

---

17   Alasdair MacIntyre, 'The Very Idea of a University: Aristotle, Newman and Us', *British Journal of Educational Studies* 57:4 (2009), 347-362, DOI: 10.1111/j.1467-8527.2009.00443.x, 348f.

18   For a more academic discussion, see Alister McGrath, *A Scientific Theology*, Vol. 2, T&T Clark, Edinburgh 2002, 228.

Haman obeys, then hurries home, devastated. But it is now time for the banquet. He is summoned, and after the meal Esther confronts the king with the implications of Haman's evil plan, that she is to be one of the victims. When she names Haman, the king stalks out in fury; Haman falls down at the knees of the queen to beg for mercy, the king returns, views Haman as assaulting the queen, and Haman's fate is sealed. He is hanged – and later his ten sons – on his own gallows.

"I wish the story ended there," said Jean.

There was still one problem. We know from the story of Daniel and Lion's Den that "the laws of the Medes and the Persians cannot be changed", and Haman's law for a pogrom on the 13th day of the 12th month still stood.

Jean's comment was, "We would just repeal a bad law."

"That wasn't how things worked. Anyhow, by this time the king had made Mordecai first minister in Haman's place, so Mordecai got a second law passed, allowing the Jews not only to defend themselves, but to annihilate anyone planning to attack them."

"And since the Jews had a pretty good idea of who was against them, there was a lot of bloodshed," added Jean, who of course knew the story well enough.

Maybe the bloodshed is just self-defence, or maybe we have the irony of Jewish people getting their revenge. We still have these two interpretations in the Middle East today. One is that Israel is seeking to make the state safe against threats of annihilation by Arab powers; the other is that Israel has moved from the weakness of being a minority in the early 20th CE to being strong enough to put the boot into the Palestinians whenever she wishes.

Mordecai is certainly the hero of the story – Esther's guardian, saviour of the king, mentor to his adopted daughter, on whom he puts pressure as the crisis unfolds. When the tables are turned, Mordecai is, then exalted from minor officialdom to high office of state (like Joseph and Daniel in others parts of the Old Testament), and celebrated at the end of the book as a wise leader and advocate for the Jews. He deserves a sonnet.

A Sonnet for Mordecai

This is how we like to build a story,
with a Haman riding fortune, thrusting
hips and ugly head, smirking, lusting
after power, hungry for the glory
to be flashed on Facebook, poured like cream
around the human berries on his plate.
He likes them red raw, by the hundredweight,
each Mordecai a hit for his esteem.

But faithful Jews to God alone bow down,
and providence is skilled at timing chance
to ca' the feet from such as Haman, stun,
hang him by the neck, and give his crown
to such as Mordecai, a circumstance
which saves his race, and profits every one.

This is a story from ancient times, but you can understand why it was important for the Jewish people to keep it in their canon of Scripture, as a reminder, or a hope, that although anti-Semitism is rife to the present day, God will find ways to protect his people.

"What about the Holocaust, then?" asked Jean. "That's why the majority of Israelis today don't believe in God. So they can celebrate Purim easily enough, as God doesn't come into it."

Esther reminds us that God is active in human affairs, even when not mentioned. As Psalm 77:19 has it, "Your way was through the sea [the Exodus rescue] . . . yet your footprints were unseen."

I wrote a poem on that psalm, and perhaps it relates the psalm to Esther and to the experience of migrants today, who like the Jews of Esther's time are trying to hold on to life and identity. It is a 'found poem', with thanks to a film by Samir Mehanovic shown at Glasgow University in 2018.

Through Our Eyes

I think of God, and I moan; I meditate, and my spirit faints . . . I am so troubled that I cannot speak. I consider the days of old, and remember the years of long ago.   Psalm 77:3-5

The razor wire cuts through me,
separating past, serrating
present, future gutted.

I walk beside the endless fence
with a thousand companions,
locked into our bleeding selves.

Assad and his army were the worst,
firing out of nowhere – even
snipers taking out the children.

We served them tea, after
the army had beaten in our door.
What is happening to respect?

My husband works away
from here; if he's late back
I fear the army took him.

My mum is sick, no blanket.
Even close to the border,
the planes come to bomb us.

The children have only the clothes
in which they fled. They remember
paradise, and cry, and cry.

I never imagined it would come
to war; nor that we'd need
a visa just to stay in Lebanon.

We don't want parcels, nothing
from you – just to return,
go back to our own country.

The world sends weapons, bombs,
then settles down to watch us;
they must want the war to stay.

The planes come. They don't
kill Daesh[19] or the Free Syrian
Army. They kill the likes of us.

Children need a home, not camp.
To those with nothing, Daesh
offers money and a future.

Why join Daesh? No one
wants to say 'I am a loser'.
Daesh offers power.

When the waters saw you, O God,
. . . the very deep trembled.
Your way was through the sea,
your path through the mighty waters,
yet your footprints were unseen.
You led your people like a flock
by the hand of Moses and Aaron.
Psalm 77:16,19-20

Migrants struggle overland,
fling themselves across the seas:
salvation wears a European face.

A Bosnian refugee gets an award
for film. At age thirteen, a Syrian
girl wins Betjeman's poetry prize.

God's way is rough, God's steps
unseen, but still the world is big
enough for every one of us.

---

19   Islamic State or ISIS.

"Who is this that darkens counsel by words without knowledge?"
Job 38:2

Chapter 3 Job

This story is rough. Why does God deal so roughly with Job, this fine, thoughtful man who goes through such terrible things? Yet the language and style is anything but rough, as the book is so well crafted. After the opening two chapters, the story is told through speeches and dialogue, and while it focuses on the injustice of life – and God – as a bonus it presents us with a theology of creation.[22]

Frances Anderson tells us, "Job is written in prose, but the speeches are in verse".[23] There is rhyme and rhythm in the poetry: e.g. Job 27:4 has two lines each ending with â, though like modern poems in English, rhyme is not a big deal; Hebrew poetry is more about ideas than sounds. In the prose, Job is a simple, good man, doing his best to cope with what happens to him. In the poetry, he is transformed into a tormented questioner of life, God and everything.

That difference between prose and poetry in Job was the inspiration for the next poem, although Job is not mentioned:

The Magic of Poetry

Humdrum to hi-fi,	Muggle to Narnian,
has-been to hero,	flat scene to full screen,
follow the honey bee	a rainbow collection
flying off manuscript.	of rhythms and glory holes
Prosy to poesy,	waiting for wordsmiths
same old to 'come with me	and shamans to stitch up
into bare beauty, step	a sharp and sweet story,
out of that dress'. Unzipped	and ravish our souls.

22 Writers as different as David Daiches (*God and the Poets*, Oxford University Press, London 1984) and Tom McLeish (*Faith and Wisdom in Science*, Oxford University Press, London 2014) both quote extensively from the book of Job.

23 *Tyndale Commentary on Job*, IVP, Leicester 1976, 37.

"Lateral thinking, I suppose," said Jean. "The only connection I can see is the word 'ravish' in the last line, that's almost fierce enough for Job. Job is not a gentle, polite story. It's rough and tough. Takes me back sixty years. Deep stuff – except for the ending, where Job magically gets everything back, even a new family, and lives happily ever after."

"Do you not think the book still makes its point, before that storybook ending?"

"With or without the ending I would have lost my faith when my father died. He was ill for about two years. I was just a teenager, and I watched him suffer. I prayed hard for him, but the cancer took him away, and my faith with it."

I wasn't expecting that. I'd known Jean for twenty years, but always as an agnostic, and somehow it had never occurred to me that she might have had a faith as a child – though of course most Scots did in those days. I tried to make some kind of suitable response, without lapsing into 'counsellor-speak', which I knew Jean would see through immediately. Being on Zoom didn't make it any easier.

"Were your family all believers when you were brought up?" I asked.

"Just nominal, like many in those days. I don't remember it making any difference, though we went to church on a Sunday."

"What about your father?"

"I don't really know. He never spoke about God."

I wasn't sure what to say next. Fortunately Jean helped me out, wise woman that she is. She went on, "One thing though, may not surprise you. I never gave up reading the Bible. It always fascinated me, even when I realised I no longer believed a lot of the things it said. I even read Job as a teenager."

"What did you make of it?"

"What I'm telling you is in words I couldn't have put together at the time, but the germ of it was there. 13:15 in the old King James Version, which is all I had then, says, 'Though he slay me, yet will I trust him'. I had this funny sense these words applied to me, even though I wasn't sure about God any more. I did still believe that life was not just chance."

"Sounds like Kipling's railway engineer, 'Predestination in the stride of yon connecting-rod.'"

As I said that I knew I was starting to be clever rather than caring. Happily Jean puts up with me. She changed the subject by giving me a challenge: "Why don't you write some more poems as a commentary on the book?"

I began with a very simple one, based on the first two chapters, the only time Satan is mentioned.

Satan Makes Himself Useful

Satan makes himself useful,
conversation partner for God,
poser of simple questions,
obedient to the letter.

Out of the presence of God,
Satan breathes a tempest
of tragedy, whisks away
animals, property, family:

makes himself more useful,
coughs on Job a virus,
leaves him as garbage,
broken but still faithful.

In the OT especially, Satan remains the servant of God, even if God's motives are different from his. After the story of Job is launched, Satan disappears. The mystery of evil and suffering is unsolved, but the OT certainly will not accept the devil as an explanation or as any kind of independent reality. The Greek thought of the NT seems a little more sympathetic to the devil as an independent power – think of the temptations of Jesus – but in the book of Revelation the devil is chained up and finally cast into the lake of fire.

One way is to say that evil is irrational, so that we cannot speak completely sensibly about it; from one angle that just gives up on the issue, but it would be fair to say that while the Bible does not explain evil, it acknowledges it, and strengthens us to fight against it.

The next poem describes the three cycles of conversation between Job and his three friends, from Chapters 4 to 26.

Cycling

Lockdown takes me round the block
of Job, for exercise;
I ride and think, I think and ride,
my thoughts go round and round.

1
How wise the words of Eliphaz,
how sharp the crit of Bildad;
jagged answers Zophar gives
to Job, left on the ground.
A vision comes to Eliphaz,
a poem to his friend,
elenchus to the third, so near
to pinning Job aground.

2
"You're just a windbag, Job my friend,
God punishes the wicked.
Pay attention to the wise,
we speak from hallowed ground.
This virus that has knocked you down
is what all sin deserves;
it eats the skin, it shrivels up
the roots beneath the ground.

3
"God is on high, beyond the clouds,
so make your prayer to him;
agree with God, and be at peace,
he'll raise you off the ground.
It's up to you, Job, take our word:
repent, and turn to God.
If not, you maggot of a man,
you'll stay down, and be ground."

. . . .

Locked down in the book of Job,
his friends have turned the key,
and left him pleading innocence
all through three cruel rounds.

"You know something, Jock? If you don't mind me saying so, I think your poetry is a little stuck in ancient ballad-with-modern-words style. Why not do something a bit more like what poets write nowadays?"

I had to think about that. Why do I seldom write in a contemporary lyric poetry style? Is it my age? Am I not reading enough? Is it my belief that poetry is more than just expressing how I feel about life? Is it incompetence? Is it just I don't have what it takes? Am I in a rut?

All that raises the question of what is one's true voice. Sometimes it takes a crisis, or at least a change of life, to uncover that distinctive voice. There are two chapters in the book of Job which embrace the three cycles of speeches like a sandwich – chapter 3 and chapter 27. They do seem to express Job's true voice in his awful situation. Could I write a poem about them in response to Jean's challenge?

Inside the Mind of Job

The anguish settles on my soul like toxic dust,
it stops my breath, it pushes
at the edges of my mind,
my life is nonsense,
surd that someone noticed
in the corner of his eye
and kicked aside, left
wriggling like a wasp half-swatted
by wiseacres knowing nothing
of the vital part it plays in the garden,
which might survive without the digging,
constant digging up of vital roots,
so now I flounder in a barrow
wheeled and emptied in a skip
with dying wasps, dead ends,
dead hopes, and zombic friends.

Assumptions riddle me like crazy bullets,
needle me with poisoned steel,
such ignorant witch-pricking,
tactics torture mind which sits with heart
in dodgems buffeted by counsellors
who pin my sins like butterflies,
flaunt my faults like fancy hats,
push pills for fake soul healing,
block my exit with their heavy boots,
tramp on the fingers of my feeling,
take a comfort break and put on trainers,
make me target as they learn kick boxing,
while I grit my rattled teeth
and hang on for my life to truth,
integrity, my reasoned right
these enemies call blight.

"What a change," said Jean. "Stream of consciousness and all that. Have you been reading Jorie Graham?"

"She *is* one of the poets I like."

"And I notice that you left out much of Chapter 7, Job calling down God's wrath on his enemies. Though I suppose you glossed it in the final line?"

Jumping to conclusions can be dire, as that poem indicates, but Jean knows how to do it graciously, and usually gets it right. Unlike Job's friends, whom the book leaves to get their comeuppance from God later on. Meanwhile, there is an interlude at Chapter 28, a hymn or poem about wisdom, which comes as a relief after the bluster and bullying of those three wise men. It majors on the image of wisdom as a priceless mineral which has to be mined at great cost – and the cost is so often paid in human lives.

Lonely Roads

Lonely the miner's path
Digging for gold, digging for coal
Digging for some victory?
More, digging for survival

Lonely the survivors walk
Children, brothers, sisters lost
Aleppo, Aberfan, the Iolaire
who adds up the human cost?

Lonely the philosopher
who lives uneasily inside us
seeking at every pithead
shafts of light to guide us

"I see you abandoned your usual punctilious punctuation," Jean said. "You really are trying to be up to date."

"I don't mind a bit of experiment. Actually I was wanting to show how the questions in Job, and inside us, keep coming up and shouldn't be shut up by a full stop."

The questions return in Chapters 29 – 31. I decided not to write a poem on those three chapters, as a reminder to myself that Job is such great poetry as it is, with God's lamp shining over Job's head before all this, his steps washed with milk, and nobles putting their hand to their mouths as Job passed by. How much we need today leaders who are "eyes to the blind, and feet to the lame", who champion the cause of the stranger, who smile upon those with no confidence! In books like this, wisdom is not an intellectual achievement, as with the Greek tradition, but practical; not only found in right dealing with people, but with the land itself; how sharply 31:38 speaks to the ecological crisis of today: "If my land has cried out against me, / and its furrows have wept together . . ."

The chorus found in Chapter 28, "But where shall wisdom be found?" and the way the chapter ends, with the fear of the Lord as true wisdom, remind us that the book of Job is part of this collection of 'wisdom books'. The same thought is found in Proverbs 1:7 and 9:10.

"The words of Job are ended" at the close of Chapter 31 – but the story has not ended. However before the climax a young man, Elihu turns up and in six whole chapters appear to repeat the platitudes of Job's three friends earlier on. Actually there is more in these chapters than meets the eye, and commentaries bring this out. One point is worth mentioning: 32:3 says in the NRSV that Elihu was not only angry with Job "because he justified himself rather than God", but with his three friends because although they had declared Job to be in the wrong they had not managed to get through to him – inferring that at the end of the discussion Job's view (that God was being unfair) held the floor. So there was more to be said, even if (like Job) we are not convinced by it.

Some have thought that the Elihu section was brought into the story by a different writer – but the six chapters are full of allusions to the earlier cycle of speeches, and are more likely to have been simply the way an old story-teller sums up what has gone before. At any rate, I decided to move on to the climax, cleverly anticipated in Elihu's closing words in Chapter 37, without offering Elihu a poem. The climax comes in two devastating chapters, 38 and 39, when the Lord appears and gives an answer to Job.

"It's not really an answer at all, is it?" was Jean's opinion.

"True in one sense. It's not a logical answer to the problem of evil and suffering, instead it's a literary answer. But it certainly is received as an answer by Job, who lays his hand on his mouth in verse 4 of Chapter 40."

"Do you think it helps anyone today?"

"Well, take that verse you remember – 'though he slay me, yet will I trust him' – that presents a view which is hard for people nowadays, but if you accept God as the mysterious hand behind all things, it becomes wonderfully comforting. At first sight, it presents God as another word for fate, but if for other reasons you have come to experience God in a personal way, it presents a faith which disaster can shake, but not destroy. We may be reduced to lament instead of praise, we may feel anger rather than peace, but God is still there, independent of how we feel."

"I hoped you were going to say God was present in our suffering, rather than behind it all," was Jean's comment.

"That is certainly more the New Testament take on suffering, especially the cross. But it's not really there in the book of Job, or in the Psalms, which take the absence of God seriously."

"If I could get a handle on how God can be both present and absent at the same time, I'd be more convinced."

"I'm not sure that we can ever get a full handle hold on God, though I do believe he can get a handle on us, grab us if you like. Remember than the universe is not like a box which you are either inside or outside of.[24] Maybe however, the cross does give us a clue, where Jesus feels the absence of God, but at the same time God is present in Jesus, experiencing that absence. Deep stuff, and I don't think I can go any further than that."

Almost Persuaded

Grab me by the nose
with scent of wild dog rose,   *Dog rose:* pleasure and pain
the love of Ruth, the pain of Job,
the scent of Song of Songs.
Touch my thirsty skin
with honeysuckle, calm   *Honeysuckle:* the bond of love
my fears with hellebore.   *Hellebore:* please allay my disquiet

Grab me by the balls
with iris, if you must,   *Iris:* promise and passion
to kill my lust for gardening
within rhyme and reason,
planting shrubs and flowers
I can name, tending trees
whose future I can tame.

Grab me by the arm
and promise me no harm,
blue violet I can pick,   *Violet:* love, faithfulness, watchfulness
some edelweiss and juniper   *Edelweiss:* courage, nobility
to help me trust the messenger   *Juniper:* chastity, eternity
and step beyond the circle
of my repertoire of sense.

---

24 This is a reference to relativity theory, which the disciples of course got a glimpse of as they struggled to understand how Jesus could actually be God – God holding the universe together yet present within it at the same time.

Grab me tight and true

with more than sharp goat's-rue,　　　*Goat's-rue:* reason

for better rough reality

beyond the mind's smooth grasp:

your sage will prove more closely true　　*Sage:* wisdom, immortality

than fact too neatly packed,

or fiction of phenomena.

"I'm glad you told me the meaning of the flowers," Jean said. "That helped me see where you were going at the end. I think you were advocating a philosophy of critical realism,[25] somewhere between literalism and instrumentalism.[26] It's where most scientists are, I suppose, but I can see how it works with religion too."

The old view of rhetoric was a triad of *logos, ethos* and *pathos*: logic, credibility and emotion. If you think of a stool, the failure of one leg (say logic) is fatal, but if you think of a rope, each strand strengthens the other. The poem is looking at all three, wondering how to trust, when reason is inadequate. The book of Job recognises that human logic, put forward by Eliphaz, Bildad, Zophar and Elihu, fails – we need a different kind of logic to deal adequately with the mystery of life. The NT takes this much further by identifying Jesus of Nazareth with the divine *logos*, the book of Job simply indicates by its final chapter its faith that things *will* work out in the end.

"It's that final chapter that gets me," Jean said again.

"We haven't got there yet. But again, the poetry of 38 – 41 is of a quality I don't think I can match."

---

25 The view of Scripture and of life which has been described as 'critical realism' is developed, for example, in McGrath 2002, 195f. The poem looks for a way to bridge fact and fiction.

26 'Literalism' – where words are taken to describe what is absolutely true. 'Instrumentalism' – where words are seen as tools to express what you want to say in order to achieve a purpose, not statements about truth.

"Well, how about simply writing your own response to it. Isn't that what most poems are anyhow, a response to something that grabs you?"

God's Gig Unplugged

You call me in, Job, because
your callous colleagues called you out.
You tell me I have lost control,
the world has fallen off the map
you drew to keep things right.

You call me in, humankind,
so look at earth, its stones, its sea,
its pigs and plants, its milk and honey,
feel its setting in the stars;
just look, salute its mystery.

You call me out, clever ones
who think it wiser to proceed
si Deus non daretur. Well,   as if God were not given
I will not quarrel, but I leave
the universe in code.

You call me out a thousand times
in rage and pain; all through the blur
of human grief you shout my name
as curse or prayer. And if you go
the way of Job, you'll find me there.

"So you do really think God might be present in Job's situation?"

"Yes, even if the book doesn't suggest it, we have a bigger worldview and are free to read things in as well as read things out.

But anyhow, even if Job's three friends locked Job down, and then Elihu threw away the key, God picked it up."

"Your language in that poem reminds me of that book that Tom McLeish wrote," Jean added. "*Faith and Wisdom in Science.*[27] He uses the book of Job more than any other part of the Bible. He sees extraordinary connections between Job and modern science as it struggles with order and chaos, and what it means to be ignorant in an ever more complex world. I must say I was heartened to discover a scientist as humble as McLeish.

I had to admit that I was reading that particular book to get ideas for the poem. Jean's intuition is uncanny. Tom McLeish was allowed to choose the name of his chair at York University (he is now professor of Natural Philosophy). Up to the 19th CE, scientists were known as 'natural philosophers', and the word 'philosophy' comes from the Greek *love of wisdom* – and hence the title of the book.

One of the marks of a true scientist is a humility before the scale and wonder of the universe. The more we know, the more we know we don't know. This comes out in the book of Job, where his three friends 'know it all', but at the climax of the book, it is God alone who knows the secrets of the world, and Job in his humble ignorance who is finally approved by God.

One of the perks of writing a book like *From Ruth to Lameantations* is that you suddenly think of poems written years ago which might fit. So I found myself thinking of the practical philosopher John Peck who died in 2016, whom the art historian Karen Mulder called "the least known best theologian in the world". When I met him in his final year of life he gave me a book he had written, *Uncommon Sense*. It inspired the poem on the next page. I was spending a few days at Madingley Hall in Cambridge, and this gave me the chance to visit him.

---

27 Oxford University Press, Oxford 2014.

Meeting John Peck after 25 years

Old meets very old and what is that about if time is instant
    yet a sack of memories, a rack of good intentions flank our space
    across the floor to where John occupies his wife's late throne, his face
    furrowed with life, lines of it whorled around bright eyebrows
        and a sparkle of intent to grace our meeting,
      as he will, but how will that unfold, I wonder,
    as an arc of understanding builds again between us,
lighting up not just a second but a life-time's passion to link tight
    cables between head and heart, belief and practice, Godward faith
    and social factors, failures, faint but still pursuing, grasping
      for a goal that's moving faster than his stumbling bones,
      louder, softer than the weak or strident over, undertones
    of preaching, writing, teaching, training, all our working life
    spent gorging on our graft, delighting in our craft
which ends up (ever so politely) dust, ashes with us in the Crem.

Old meets very old and what is that about if time is stretched
    into eternity and every moment lit with meaning in the mind
    of God with whom the mighty sweep of evolution is no blind
      procession but a thoughtful, elegant, purposed process
      where God waits, fascinated, to see where it is leading,
    since God's faith is more reliable than ours, and we should know
    that, since the faith of Christ (not ours) is what survives
and brings our ashes back to life undreamt of . . . but now back to John,
    his 91st birthday card from children fostered or adopted,
      with his thank you poem displayed upon a cabinet
      beside his daughter Edith googling for a verse or two
    I mentioned, like 'the men of Issachar knew what Israel should do
    and when they ought to do it.' That's when John staggered
    to a busy shelf and found his book *Uncommon Sense*, and gifted me
this piece of past, no light-weight understanding here.

Old meets very old and what is that about when time stands still:
    I am on the doorstep, waiting till a shuffling voice intones 'I'm here!'
    A key turns slowly, lets the 'grandfather of Greenbelt Festival' appear,
        unsteady but committed to this tryst which has to pick up
        after quarter of a century of busy absence, friendship drifted
    until time tapped us on the forehead, and I hear again
    that gravel of a voice that yanked a thousand students
out of slumber into life and social action, with a lab technique
    that let this spark of understanding arc from God to lecture room
    and burn away our gristled reasons for inaction. He blesses me,
        the very old prays for the old, but what is age
        when time is but a brief dimension of a stage
    of who knows what save God, although we picture God
    as old and shuffling, when we ought to think of music, dance,
advance of science. Howanever: God (like John) has such a lived-in face.

Jean said she liked meeting someone with a lived-in face; it would certainly describe Job. I told her about another commentary I liked – John Goldingay's *Job for Everyone*.[28] When he was asked to write it, the author had just lost his wife after she had been ill with multiple sclerosis for 43 years, which gave the book a special authenticity. I wanted to see what Goldingay made of the last chapter of Job.

    Unlike many who felt the last chapter too easy, he liked the ending of Job. In fact he turned the argument right round. Accepting that most people find the ending unrealistic, Goldingay suggested that a happy ending is precisely what we need, because so many of our stories end unhappily. The NT in particular affirms resurrection, a good ending to human life, and it is remarkable to find that kind of ending affirmed also in the book of Job – let's be thankful for it! I would add that the ending is easier to accept when you realise the whole thing is a story, and that Job's wife didn't really have to bear another ten children.

---

28 SPCK, London 2013.

Whatever you think of Job getting "twice as much as he had before", he did get something else of huge importance – God declares in Chapter 42 that Eliphaz and his two friends had "not spoken of me what is right, as my servant Job has". One of the most painful things to bear is false accusation; no wonder that has a whole commandment to itself in Exodus 20. It is bad when the accuser knows the accusation is false, as in the 'show trials' of Communist regimes. It is even worse when the accusers believe the accusation is true, and only the accused knows it is false, but is under pressure to believe she is in fact guilty, as in the witch-finding trials of the 17th century (or some modern miscarriages of justice), and in any period when the accuser suffers from a mental delusion. That led to a final poem.

Desperate Doggerel

What do you say
to an old rag doll
pulled out to play,
battered, scorned,
come what may,
covered in kisses,
stroked one day,
dressed to the nines,
stripped to grey,
kicked in a corner
and thrown away?

What do you make
of Job's three friends,
joining the wake
on his ash heap grave
with an ugly take
on truth pinned down,
integrity fake,
his hope misplaced,
all sheer heartbreak?
Three nasty bites
from a skanky snake.

What do you do
at the end of the day
with a miserable crew,
false comforters
who take Job through
theological hell,
leave him to stew?
God sorts things out
with a true world view,
sends Job's three friends
to the end of the queue.

"An honest title!" said Jean.

"Yes," I replied. "I want to make a simple comment on the book of Job – different from the complex poetry of the book. It's about the hell of false accusation. That's bad enough when it comes from someone who does it deliberately; it's even worse when you get the rag doll treatment from someone in a state of theological paranoia, someone who thinks they are bringing you love and in fact are flinging judgment in your face, unaware of what they are up to."

"That makes me think of Christ's word on the cross: 'Father, forgive them, for they know not what they do.'"

"Anyhow, God told Job to pray for his three friends, and God said he would accept Job's prayer. And if God accepted Job's prayer, then surely God accepted his Son's prayer."

"The name of the Lord is a strong tower; the righteous run into it and are safe." Proverbs 18:10

Chapter 4 Proverbs

Another 'wisdom book', but ever so different from Job. Where Job is visionary and full of angst, Proverbs is humdrum and treats life as a classroom, not a theatre. One of my teachers, Norman Porteous, used to say that "we need the Old Testament when the New Testament seems too good to be true", and one might follow that by saying "we need the book of Proverbs when the book of Job has left us black and blue", or simply by saying it's an easier read (if less dramatic). At first glance, it seems dull, no different from common sense sayings in any culture, and then, suddenly you come on something like 25:21, "If your enemies are hungry, give them bread to eat . . ." While that is exactly what Elisha organised in 2 Kings 6:22-23, it is so different from the teaching of other ancient cultures.[29]

Perhaps one reason for that is the man who is claimed as the author at the start, Solomon. Job was a wise and wealthy man who learned even more wisdom through suffering, and discovered that worldly wealth was for God to give or withhold. Solomon was a wise and wealthy man who never lost it. There are swings and roundabouts to the different proverbs, but they are as tame and as safe as the book of Job is wild and scary. They are about every day wisdom, and however 'ordinary' they sound, knowing and obeying them goes a long way toward social cohesion and individual well-being.

"Proverbs was written for me," said Jean.

"Whatever do you mean?" I asked.

---

29   C.S. Lewis, *Christian Reflections*, Geoffrey Bles, Reading 1967, 116.

"Remember how I told you I lost my faith in a God who answered prayer? I never lost my faith in the value of religion. None of this contemporary 'spirituality not religion' for me. Although I stopped going to church regularly I could see how people found its teaching gave them a direction in life. And I knew the Bible was a kind of life guide in its own way – it spoke to me, even though I was not sure about the God who was supposed to have inspired it. I kept reading it, not least the book of Proverbs. I was still young, and Proverbs was written for the young."

"'Young men' would be the translation of Proverbs 1:4 in your day, I suppose, Jean – though nowadays we have just 'young', which is just as well."

I suddenly remembered what I was once told in Tanzania, how a generation ago teenagers used to hold competitions, to see who could remember the most proverbs. Come to that, when I was young we did the same thing with nursery rhymes as well as riddles.

Tae Mak Hauflins Lang-Heidit

"Kitendawili!" (Here's a riddle)
"Tega" (Catch me if you can) – Swahili saying

A wey o flytin – tell yin hauf,	*competing half*
see if the ither kens the lave.	*rest*
Nae glaur fechting, jist fire lichting,	*mud wrestling*
gien yir ken an wit a have.	*knowledge wisdom heave*
Darg an Hainins	*work savings*
A penny hained: a penny gained	*saved*
Pleuch deep: whil sluggards sleep	*plough*
Borrae an bigg: blaw-oot an beg	*borrow build*
A greedy ee: ne'er gat a fou wame	*eye full womb*
Laith tae bed: laith tae rise	*late*
Oer muckle at ae thing: is gude for naething	

Kin an Friens   *family friends*
Friens are lik fiddle-strings: they maunna be screwed ower ticht
Aa thit's sayed in the kitchie: shouldna be tauld in the ha
Is the auld cock craws: the young cock larns
Atween three an thirteen: thraw the woodie whan it's green
A wile goose: ne'er laid tame eggs
Auld tods: need nae tutors   *foxes*

Ither Saylns
The day his een: the nicht his lugs   *eyes   ears*
He thit has bit ae ee: maun tent it weel   *take care of*
He thit sleeps wi dugs: maun rise wi fleas
Thirs nane sae blin: as thaim that winna see
Wit ance bocht: is wirth it twice taught
Poets an painters: hae leave tae lee   *lie*
Ah cudnae pass ower yon blenk tae a scriever,   *wink writer*
fur irony's fun in the guid buik an aa,
and thir's mony a byway thit leads tae the highway
o wisdom and truth, gin ye're earn an nae daw.   *eagle juckdaw*

"Is education more about drawing stuff out of pupils than putting it in, do you think?" I asked Jean, knowing how experienced she was as a teacher. I thought that if we were looking at a book like Proverbs, this would be a good time to get her talking about teaching.

"It's both of course," said Jean, and then went back to the poem. "I thought teaching might be a kind of 'byway', as I really wanted to keep studying; I must admit I fancied myself as a professor, just because there were hardly any women with chairs in those days," said Jean.

This time I didn't interrupt. She went on, "But I discovered being a school-teacher was my calling; in my day at least it was deeply satisfying; all the form-filling and protecting your back only came in at the end of my career. I counted myself lucky to get the chance of early retirement."

"So you believe in divine guidance?"

"I wouldn't call it divine. More like discovering who you are meant to be."

Jean's insight came through daily life and its discoveries. We work things out as we go along. That fits in with the book of Proverbs, but our 'going along' must be diligent.

"Jean," I said. "Do you remember I went to study poetry for a week in Spain, at a converted farmhouse in the Sierra Nevada? I wrote a poem about that famous verse in Proverbs 6, 'Think of the ant, you sluggard!'"

A Proverb Reconsidered

Tracking wild across the Sierra Nevada,
the ants are in God's eye, a little armada
of twitching purpose, joyfully numbered,
since one ant is worth a thousand elephants
in heaven's economy. Even one dumb bird
is not an oxymoron, and God (for instance)
puts a single anthill on the same sure
footing as a skyscraper, because they share
the solid earth, and need the same pure
air. With God one single petal is as fair
as any grand bouquet, two millimetres
rank beside two thousand metres.

How to recalibrate our thought
is something urgent that we ought
to do. For if an insignificant ant
can ferry something twenty times its size
with giant energy, keep constant
witness to God's algebra, surprise
us all with tricks of geo-engineering,

then we need to get down on our knees
and see through God's own lens, peering
at these little creatures and their cities,
nests of enterprise; for God is adamant,
and tells us slugs, "Observe the ant!"

God is the author of wisdom, but wisdom, created right at the beginning by God (8:22), is the focus of Proverbs. And if 'wisdom' sounds a bit grand, think of 'tips for a good life'. Practical philosophy.

Chapter 8 is the only chapter in the book which waxes poetic about wisdom and where it comes from. It follows several chapters on the dangers of violence and loose women – like virtually all writings of the period, it is a male viewpoint. John Goldingay points out that the book was used for training those who would be leaders in the civil service of the day, and exposed to particular temptations. In our day of more equal opportunities, women need to reverse the genders named in the book.[30] But I guess Jean was doing that anyway.

Churches have a reputation for going on and on about sex, and ignoring other things. If that cap fits, we should wear it, but the book of Proverbs – which is written for an age of small town family life – recognises how important it is, and that when men (and women) get things wrong in this area it plays havoc with family life. None of the modern nothing-buttery, the idea that sex is 'nothing but' play between two people (although Proverbs 5:19 does mention the play in passing).

The Song of Songs has plenty about sex as play, but Proverbs knows it is more than that, because people live in families and neighbourhoods. Wisdom is set as a father's instruction (1:8), and the Lord's gift (2:6).

---

30 John Goldingay, *Proverbs, Ecclesiastes and the Song of Song for Everyone*, SPCK, London 2014, 25.

Alone

He loved her, lost her
in court, and passing time.

She sought him, found him
too late, lost him again.

We learn to live alone,
lamenting past and present.

"What possessed you to write that poem?" asked Jean. "We've left Job behind. The book of Proverbs is optimistic, and that poem has not a word of hope in it."

"I was thinking of fathers today, and their pain – so often separated from their family. Proverbs may be optimistic on the whole, but when it speaks of people being lost because of folly it is realistic."

"But the point of Job is that we may end up lost even in our wisdom!"

"For every wise Job there are not a few foolish fathers. I think we need the wisdom to know when to go to Job, and when to stay with Proverbs."

Which we are now doing, in Chapter 3 to be precise. What is striking is the fact that the Lord, 'Yahweh' as it is usually now written (same as 'Jehovah' in the past) the special covenant name for God, is mentioned five times in eight verses. In the rest of the book, the Lord is mentioned, but not so often. With Job, at the start and finish, we had this personal name, 'the Lord', but through all the cycles of speeches, we had the more distant 'God', or 'the Almighty'.

"So Proverbs and Job have something in common!" said Jean.

"I suppose so. And there they are in the same Bible! I could write a poem about that."

Job and Proverbs

'Consider Job,' began the Adversary,
seeing how he honoured God, accepted
discipline, his godly fear and trust.
'Consider Job,' continued Satan smugly,
'knock away his knowing faith in proverbs,
show him human wisdom is a myth,
plague his skin and break his nose,
see how deep his goodness goes.'

'You may do these things, ungodly servant,
I don't practise cursing humankind!'
The script agreed, the narrative proceeds,
dismantling trust, replacing holy fear
with dark despair, a mockery of honour,
discipline distorted in the fists
of friends. Thus Satan gave offence
to Job, and to proverbial sense.

So far, maybe too much wordy prose,
juxtaposition showing clever things
like intertextuality, the way
two genres click their heels to one another,
dance so brilliantly across the floor
of wisdom.
                    Pause. Grow wise.
                              Replace whatever
books you have upon your shelves,
and read the scripture texts themselves.

"My brother liked Proverbs 3" said Jean. 'Once he made a collage of
all the important things in his life, and stuck that text underneath,
'In all your ways acknowledge him, and he will make straight your
paths.'"

I remembered the course Jean said her brother's life took, and thought about crooked paths, but kept my mouth shut. After all, if intertextuality means anything, we can add in a few parables, like the story of the two brothers in Luke 15. Maybe the story of a sister and a brother. It came good at the very end.[31]

"Jean, this is what happens when I try to write a poem. I get carried away somewhere else. In fact it happens just reading the Bible. I'm fascinated with the way the different books fit together."

"OK, but let's stick to Proverbs in the meantime. There's one verse in Chapter 4 which really contradicts the story of Job.

The path of the righteous is like the light of dawn,
which shines brighter and brighter until full day."

"It contradicts more than Job," I said. "It contradicts our natural experience of life – birth is like dawn, but death is like sunset. If Proverbs is supposed to be down to earth, that verse is like a spaceship always in sunlight, but on the dark side of the moon."

"Perhaps it is because wisdom is supposed to be eternal."

Jean has this extraordinary knack of coming out with profound stuff. I often think that while her head may be agnostic, her heart has always been somewhere else. I wonder if the two will come together. Meantime, we went on to Chapter 8, and started talking about Lady Wisdom, since the Hebrew word *hokmah* is feminine, like the word for spirit, *ruach*. The Greeks had a *goddess* of wisdom, Sophia.

"Jean," I said, "John Goldingay now talks about Ms. Wisdom being created before anything else, to be God's co-worker in creation."

"You and I don't have to be as politically correct as that."

"Indeed – but talking of wisdom as a lady does give an impression of leisured gentility which is not in the text. Wisdom is the brains and the powerhouse of creation, according to Proverbs 8, a 'master worker' – but another translation is 'little child', and if

31 The full story is in *From Cosmos to Canaan*.

you put those together you get a wonderful picture of God having fun making the world."

There had to be a playful poem about that:

Godly Play

God did a risk assessment,
wrote the quantum book,
threw in evolution,
brewed a cosmic soup;
God took his time, and left
the human race a lot
of space to grow their wisdom;
it isn't finished yet.

"I like the idea of us growing in wisdom. Confucius was into that. He took his disciples with him on his travels, so they could learn from the problems they met."

"Interesting that there are now thousands of schools in China teaching his ideas, just fifty years after he was denounced by Mao as an enemy of the people."

While much of the Old Testament book of Proverbs dates from before the time of Confucius, his sayings (in the *Analect*, Jean told me) may have been put together round about the same time as the book of Proverbs took the form we now have. The search for the "house of wisdom" is a worldwide, time long search.

"Why is Wisdom's house in Chapter 9 built with seven pillars?" asked Jean.

"I don't know," I said, "except that seven is a round number, which is why you have the expression back in Chapter 6, 'there are six things the Lord hates, seven that are an abomination to him.'"

Proverbial List Poem

Proud eyes God hates,	More years God waits,
loud tongues God hates,	for this God waits,
all folk who lie	to see on earth
and rile their kin;	his own blood line;
dead hearts God hates	now still God waits,
red hands God hates	how long God waits
and feet that put	for me to change
the boot right in.	and make it mine.

From Chapter 10, nearly 13 chapters are devoted to a collection called "the proverbs of Solomon". Like "the psalms of David", they may not all come from Solomon, or he may simply have collected them himself. And like proverbs in any language, they can contradict each other (e.g. 10:10 and 11:12). 15:27 commends 'hating bribes', but 18:16 (with 21:14) accepts that a gift "opens doors". Just as one person's terrorist may be another's freedom fighter, so one man's bribe may be another's gift. You need wisdom to fit a proverb to the right situation, which is why a proverb in the mouth of a fool is "like a thorn bush waved by a drunk man".

People as different as John Wesley and Andrew Carnegie taught that you should decide a modest amount to live on, and give away the rest. The book of Proverbs also commends "a little with the fear of the Lord", and rates "a dinner of vegetables where love is" above a banquet (15:16-17).

Nano-poetry

Lord, make me a nano-poet,
eyes wide open to that dewdrop
glistening on the brassica,
ready for the chef to cut
and cook a simple dish to fit
that fresh proverbial diet.

Lord, make me a nano-poet,
ears cocked for each low note
you sound with my fumbling bow
that strokes the nervous strings
of this stumbling Stradivarius
you dwell in by your Spirit.

Lord, make me a nano-poet,
senses touched by just a hint
of recipe and composition,
music, feasting, wonderment
at what you grow within
this tiny plot; the bugs all know it.

"Do you remember E. F. Schumacher and *Small is Beautiful*?" asked Jean.

"Indeed I do – and the subtitle, 'A Study of Economics as if People Mattered'. Yet we still measure the value of a country by its GDP."

"What about the idea of a happiness index?"

"I quite like the 'Happy Planet Index', even though Britain doesn't score well. Proverbs has plenty to say about happiness. Like the cheerful heart in 17:22."

Court Jester

"A cheerful heart is excellent medicine"
– as King Solomon told his court comedian,
though maybe all those pleasure gardens,
horses, women, gold shares helped a bit,
in spite of those severe disclaimers
in Ecclesiastes; but then, jesters
are quite famous for the wisdom
lurking cheerfully beneath their wit.

"I noticed that you connected one poem with Job, and now this one with Ecclesiastes. Surely the three books are very different?"

"Jean, the style, even the genre is quite different. But all three are books about wisdom. There is a Hebrew phrase, 'the words of the wise' which only occurs four times in the Bible, twice in Proverbs and twice in Ecclesiastes. Those who study them should begin with the fear of the Lord in Proverbs 1:7, and end with keeping God's commandments in Ecclesiastes 12:13."[32]

"I thought an expression like 'the fear of the Lord' was now banned as theologically incorrect. I would never use it with children."

"I understand why. You could substitute 'healthy respect'. But there's something in it that our generation wanted to hang on to. Remember how Mr Beaver talked about Aslan, when Lucy asked if he was safe. 'Safe? . . . Who said anything about safe? Course he isn't safe. But he's good.'"[33]

"I would love to believe that. I know you do. But the evidence is against it. If God exists, he is not good if he lets so much nasty stuff happen – on his watch, one would have to say. I believe in goodness, I've seen it in people I admire, and I can find it in Proverbs. But if you took the word 'God' or 'Lord' away from the book, it would be just the same."

I had to agree with Jean, that if Proverbs was all we had, God would be a bit redundant – except for that one verse, "The fear of the Lord is the beginning of wisdom". You'd need to leave that one out. I knew it would not be wise to argue with Jean, so (as often) I put my argument, and a bit of passion, into a prayer poem, or it might be better to say an enquiry poem. I had just been watching a TV adaptation of Hardy's *Tess of the D'Urbervilles*. Thomas Hardy was a good poet as well as a good novelist.

---

32 Kathleen Farmer, *Who Knows What is Good?*, Eerdmans/Handsel, Grand Rapids 1991, 3.

33 C.S. Lewis, *The Lion, the Witch and the Wardrobe*, Geoffrey Bles, London 1950, 77.

The Good Author

So: we dub Tom Hardy, Austen, Shakespeare,
C.S. Lewis, all this gang of writers
'very good'.
We praise them, cite their characters, admire
their hand and footwork, skill to tease our minds
and wrench our guts, hearts at the mercy
of their mood.

Is such an author good at more than words?
Does she connect with more than we can see,
and does that count
as anything that changes heaven and earth,
breathes goodness into Glasgow, breaks a curse,
turns goddamn doom to godly blessing, just
the tiniest amount?

We glibly spell this word with top case A,
and lay on God the mess of humankind
– a thankless task.
If only God did more than write the script,
but somehow slipped onto the stage, and left
a witness somewhere in the human play,
that's worth an ask.

"Who exactly are you arguing with in that poem – if it is a poem?"
enquired Jean.

I decided to give a very honest answer. "I started by arguing
with you, and I ended up arguing with myself."

"I'm quite touched by that," said Jean, "but I need a comfort
break."

While she was away, I kept on thinking about the author's
part in the play. It's a well known slant on the idea of incarnation,
but I was writing on the Old Testament. Way back on Exodus I had

written about Moses and the face of God,[34] and here in Proverbs 15:2 we have "the eyes of the Lord are in every place". There are other places where you have the hands of God doing stuff, and the feet of God walking places. Picture language, or more than that?

When we resumed, Jean drew my attention to the second use of "the words of the wise" in Proverbs, half way through Chapter 22. "There is one verse I have heard often at funeral services, at the end of that chapter. 'Do you see those skillful in their work? They will serve kings.'"

"I used that verse at the funeral of a joiner who lived in Prestonpans. I visited him a few times before he died, and he showed me an extraordinary tool he had, a 'Granny Tooth' router, which was a very narrow plane for cutting a groove. He lived not far from Port Seton, where the Scots painter John Bellany was brought up. Bellany once painted a picture of his granny, lying in bed with her Bible, and I wrote this poem:

A Granny Tooth

I thought of the old lady
on the Bellany canvas
as I cradled the router
in my palm, felt it stroke
the warm wood, steel
on skin, as hard and soft
as a cat's paw.
              The tooth,
the tooth was ancient,
firm as the hills
across the Forth,
full of the old wisdom.

---

34 In the poem 'God's Life Space', see *From Cosmos to Canaan*, pp. 75-6.

The tooth had eyes
for the fashions of oak,
the curves of rosewood,
the marks of mahogany.
                    The tooth:
sharp set for the groove,
a blade as fierce
as her memory
of water crashing
on the boat shore
where the men
did not come back.

"Bellany painted a lot of canvases at Port Seton," I said, "and also at Eyemouth, where nearly two hundred fishermen died in the great storm of 1881."

"I like the idea of the tooth being 'full of the old wisdom'. Wisdom in the things we make, as well as in the world around us."

"That takes us a bit beyond the book of Proverbs, I suppose, except for that bit in Chapter 8 where Lady Wisdom (I can't quite take *Ms.* Wisdom) is linked to creation."

"She's probably the closest I can get to the idea of God."

We left it there for the moment. By now we had got nearer the end of Proverbs, and were looking at further collections of sayings. Sharp stuff, like putting a knife to your throat if you have a big appetite and get invited to a meal with a ruler. And sayings which Jesus picked up and reshaped in his parables, like being invited to a banquet and choosing a humble place, or not laying up treasure on earth. Earlier on, 10:25 may have sparked that story about the foolish man who built his house upon the sand. That gave me a line for another reflective poem, maybe a prayer.

Jesus, son of wisdom:
> taught by Mary in Egypt
> taught by the wise in the temple
> taught by Joseph in workshop
taught by Proverbs in Scripture

Jesus, sum of wisdom:
> taught by the wind of the Spirit
> taught by the call of the desert
> taught by the flowers of the field
> taught by the mind of God

Talking of sums, Agur son of Jakey has Chapter 30 all to himself, and he is fond of the numbers two, three and four. He begins by confessing his ignorance. Goldingay tell us his name is related to "resident alien" and so he may well be saying, "What do I know about the world – I'm just passing through!"[35] But Agur goes on to make some pertinent observations. I like the "two things" he asks of God (which turn out to be three, just as elsewhere three turns out to be four):

> Remove far from me falsehood and lying;
> give me neither poverty nor riches;
> feed me with the food that I need.
> or I shall be full and deny you,
> and say "Who is the Lord?"
> or I shall be poor, and steal,
> and profane the name of my God.

Proverbs closes with an alphabet acrostic,[36] the ode to a capable wife – a purple passage for funerals (but not weddings!), even though it presents a woman as running a home entirely by herself on minimal sleep while her husband sits in state "at the gate", the place where elders would meet to rule the roost.

---

35 Goldingay 2014, 146.

36 A poem where each line starts with a successive letter of the Hebrew alphabet.

"I have no problem with that," said Jean. "In the context of ancient life, it makes perfect sense, and we have no business judging ancient documents by modern criteria."

I think Jean would have qualified for Proverbs 31 if it had been a poem in praise of single women, as they deserve. And a comment like that indicates she would not be 'woke' enough to rename the David Hume Tower at Edinburgh University, simply because the authorities discovered that Hume's comments on slavery were mixed, like others of his day.

"A threefold cord is not quickly broken." Ecclesiastes 4:12

Chapter 5   Ecclesiastes

We expect different, even contradictory proverbs for different occasions – think of "many hands make light work" as against "too many cooks spoil the broth". We don't expect a book written by a single author to contradict itself – but Ecclesiastes does, often. Wisdom is excellent but also vexatious (2:13 and 1:18); money is unsatisfying, but it also meets every need (5:10 and 10:19). However these different perspectives are part of the overall message of Ecclesiastes – life is complicated, absurd and frustrating. Things get forgotten (1:11).[35] An epilogue at the end of Chapter 12 then reminds us that even if life is like that, we should fear God and keep his commands.

"Who do *you* think wrote the book?" asked Jean.

"The name Qohelet gets translated as Teacher, Mr Preacher, Observer, Churchman, Philosopher, but no one knows for sure. Although Qohelet claims to be son of David and king in Jerusalem, the book is cynical about kings, and the language is much later than Solomon's time. It's a bit like some of the David Psalms, and the wisest thing to say may be something like, 'think Solomon when you read this.'"[36]

"Was the author a real person, using a false name?"

"No one knows. Sometimes in Hebrew it is is 'the qohelet', sometimes just 'Qohelet'. That's why it's often translated as 'the Teacher.'"

---

35   Robert Fyall gives Vashti in the book of Esther as an example of someone airbrushed out of history (*Ruth, Esther, Ecclesiastes, Song of Songs and Lamentations*, BRF, Oxford 2005, 48) – hence the poem on page 14.

36   See Peter Enns, *Ecclesiastes*, Eerdmans, Grand Rapids 2011, 19.

"The expression 'nothing new under the sun' is still with us more than two millennia later. Do you have a poem on that?"

"More or less. Wind, not sun. And I have 'Preacher', not 'Teacher'."

Listen to the Wind

"Round and round goes the wind . . ." Ecclesiastes 1:6

We've gone this dismal way before.
The flu that swept across the world
snuffed out the cries of millions weakened
by that war to end all wars.

The minds and knees that crushed George Floyd,
Sheku Bayoh, revolving queues
of roughed up coloured folks belong
to fellow humans, not to droids.

Our eyes are weary with TV,
our lungs are choked with news that blows
us gossip, breezy jokes, the latest
bit of data. Zapper, please.

So comes that red band needle blight,
honey fungus, ash dieback,
sudden death for ancient oaks,
and people say their last good nights.

Listen to the wind. You know
its breath, its songs of something older,
something wise; it says enough,
Preacher, as it goes.

"Can I see that in print?" asked Jean. So I put it on screen share. She looked at it for a minute, and said, "OK, I see what you are up to – you have rhymes or half-rhymes trundling verse by verse all the way through!"

I was pleased she had spotted one of the techy bits, though I had rather hoped she would comment on racism and the environment. But that's the thing about poetry, it catches people different ways.

"The other word that people remember is 'vanity.'"

"All three words for emptiness come together in Chapter 2," I replied, "'all is vanity and a chasing after wind, and there is nothing to be gained under the sun.'"

Qohelet spoke of vanity in the sense of meaninglessness rather than pride. The Hebrew word comes 38 times in this book, compared with 35 times in the whole of the rest of the Old Testament. It means 'just a puff of air', but thinking of 'puff', I did write a short poem on the other sense of 'vanity' in English:

Puff

The little smile of inside knowledge
at a conversation of inferiors.

The bigger smile of real achievement,
indicating how one's skill pays off.

The little buzz of quick inclusion
in the gatherings that really matter.

The bigger buzz of reputation
trailed so modestly, and traced to source.

These little puffs of vanity
just etch a grin upon the devil's face.

There are patches of light in the book. After Qohelet complains how futile life is, how wine, women and song do not satisfy, how all our work is a waste of time, how even at night we get no rest, how we take nothing with us when we die, at 2:24 he suddenly says that with God we can enjoy our food and our work, and mentions wisdom and knowledge and joy. But these shifts from darkness to light, and then maybe back again, are true to life. It's that faithful witness to how things really can be that makes this a great book for preachers today.

However, it goes deeper than that. Eugene Peterson remarks that in the religious marketplace, lots of people are being offered cheap miracles and easy answers to life situations. The book of Ecclesiastes is there to warn us that they don't bring us what they promise.[37] There are miracles, and there are answers, but they don't come off the peg, they come through wisdom, and through unexpected and certainly undeserved grace. Qohelet will hint at this later, when he writes, "You do not know the work of God, who makes everything." (11:5)

Fate and Freedom

So you've tried it on already?
The shoe fits, for a while, if you can afford it,
but don't collect shoes, or women, or wealth:
for a collectible, try wisdom.

And keep your mouth shut.
Look, and learn – though knowledge hurts.
Pain and pleasure come and go, but proverbs
make you smile awhile.

Enjoy being young, and alive.
That's the time to know the God who made you.
Don't lose your head in books or beer,
and hedge your bets a bit.

Are things just getting worse?
You must be getting old and crabbit. OK,
but wisdom beats nostalgia every time.
Ask more intelligent questions.

---

37 Eugene H. Peterson, *Five Smooth Stones for Pastoral Work*, Eerdmans, Grand Rapids 1992, 149-152.

Let God into your mind.
God can handle bad stuff better than you;
God doesn't need the devil for an excuse;
God will sort things out one day.

It may well be written:
"A time for this, a time for that."
Think written *up*, not written *down*
as by *a moving finger*.

Animals and humans die.
We share our genes with mice and monkeys,
conscious of our limits. God, give us
please, more light on living.

We hang up mental pictures
and they go and surf our brain waves.
Rob Pinsky's *dire one* or *desired one*[38]
is left an open question.

"I know Pinksky's poem," said Jean, "Good choice. All about God's ambiguity, appearing in conflicting roles – wound and medicine, saviour and sentencer. It suits Ecclesiastes, though if I remember right, he has a reference to the wisdom figure in Proverbs 8."

There's Jean again. Her knowledge of poetry is impressive. Mind you I was writing about the different sides of life, rather than God. That passage in Ecclesiastes 3, there is a time for this, and a time for that.

"I know Ecclesiastes 3 is often read at funerals," said Jean, "but if Qohelet means 'the Preacher', do you get sermons on the book today?"

"I love preaching on Ecclesiastes," I said immediately. "So many memorable sayings. Take this one in Chapter 3: 'God has put a sense of past and future into their minds, yet they cannot

---

38 From his poem *'Ode to Meaning'*.

find out what God has done from the beginning to the end.' In simple terms, that verse invites a three-part sermon: the way we reach out to try and understand time and eternity, second how we can't find out more than that by ourselves, and then third the light that God has given us."

"Do you know, Jock, it was Ecclesiastes that made me want to study philosophy in particular. Job kept alive in me the sense there just might be meaning to life, Proverbs showed me the value of morality and religious practice, but Ecclesiastes fascinated me with the ideas of meaning and meaningless."

"Jean, I think you were a very unusual teenager!"

"Teenagers are not all the same. You soon learn that as a teacher. And in the sixth form you have this privilege of discussing ideas, and what life might mean."

"Surely in your day philosophy was dominated by people like A.J. Ayer, who reduced it to language and learning to think clearly?"

"Not so much in Scotland. We always kept the idea that language was more than just an instrument to convey what was in one person's mind to another, the belief that somehow what we say, however flawed, might have some connection to a reality beyond us. That's why I never gave up on God altogether, even though I could never find him."

If in Chapter 3 meaning is elusive, death is certain. It comes to animals, it comes to people, so is there any difference? In the 19th century, this was one reason why Darwin and the science which followed him was controversial. If we are descended from apes, are we no more than animals? Jean was familiar with these debates, and although she called herself an agnostic, she knew perfectly well that evolution was a theory that led to incredible wonder at the complexity of things, and that if there was a creation, it made creation such a wonderful and appropriate way for God to do things, giving a new dimension to ideas like freedom and order, and that final statement in Genesis 1, God saw that it was good, and took his rest – rest in that context not meaning putting his feet up, but taking charge of all things in the cockpit of the cosmos. At least, that was how the ancients saw God ruling in his universal temple, and it doesn't seem out of pace today.[39]

Gentle Death

I remember how St Francis spoke of death,
as gentle, and I think of beastly killing fields,
of deadly viruses, of forests felled and loss of habitat,
of polar melt, of energy and entropy,
of grisly ends to man and beast alike.

But then, unlike my brother animals,
my sister creatures, I can hear a word beyond
these carnal curbs, a voice which calls me home. I have a mind
to pick and choose an unforeseen conclusion,
bound by gentle faith to things unseen.

"I hope you don't think that being able to reason makes you different from animals and birds. Crows reason. Some disabled folk can't."

"Fair point, Jean. That's a poem of testimony, not a testament of difference. The real difference seems to be that humans can reach beyond our animal life, this groping through a curtain of past and future that Qohelet talks about in 3:11, our capacity for imagination,[40] maybe our sense of eternity as some versions translate it.

---

39 See, for example, Jon D. Levenson, 'The Temple and the World', *Journal of Religion, Vol. 64 no. 3* (July 1984), 288, or more generally John Walton, *The Lost World of Genesis One*, IVP Downers Grove 2009.

40 Iain McGilchrist links this to the right hemisphere of the brain in *The Master and his Emissary*, Yale University Press, London 2009, 127.

Imagination is under-rated or even dismissed as 'unreal'. In one of his plays, the atheist Bernard Shaw had (we might say) the imagination to invent a dialogue between Joan of Arc and the Grand Inquisitor; the latter says, "Joan, these voices you hear – it's just your imagination!" Quick as a flash, Joan replies, "Of course. That's how God speaks to us."

Which is not to say the imagination cannot play tricks. Faith uses the imagination but is not dependent on it. Good religion has always made a distinction between the evidence for faith and the way of faith; in Christianity, both involve the work of Christ and the Spirit, the purpose of God and the reality of incarnation, foreshadowed in one way or another by the witness of the OT. The writings of Ecclesiastes may seem like a challenge to faith, but they too are included within the testimony, like the psalms of complaint and despair. Faith makes room for this kind of doubt. The OT is hospitable to enquiry.

I thought of poems I had written on two Psalms, and showed them to Jean.

Subversive Submission

"You will break them with a rod of iron" Psalm 2:9

Does God ever plant questions,
or simply tell us not to quest?

Is God familiar with irony,
or just with iron rods?

Might God do cynicism,
or only not do sin?

Are these legit enquiries,
and not illicit queries?

May we dismiss crass kowtowing,
but kiss God's temple feet?

Tanka for the Passing Guest

"I am your passing guest" Psalm 39:12

Each day a dice cup

shaking sunshine or shadow;

each prayer a hiccup

bouncing questions off the wall

that hides me from the future.

Poems like these appealed to a retired teacher, so Jean responded, "I can imagine a conversation with God where a person begins, 'God, I have a question', and God replies, 'Be my guest'. In fact I used the idea of conversation quite a lot in RE lessons."

"Of course we don't actually live life in this kind of armchair, quietly reflecting on issues that might or might not arise. Our questions arise in agonised situations, for ourselves and other people. And often we find that instead of giving us a neat answer, God just asks a question back at us."

"I sometimes tried to do that a teacher," said Jean. "But pupils under the pressure of exams usually wanted answers, not more questions."

Life is a very different kind of exam, and Chapter 4 introduces other things that are part of life. The tears of the oppressed, with nobody to comfort them. The wisdom of avoiding both laziness and overwork. The value of friends – two are better than one, three give the strength of a cord with three strands. Then comes the reality of *coups d'état* – perhaps the writer is thinking of the history of the northern kingdom of Israel. Yet the chapter returns to 'vanity and a chasing after wind' at its close.

Today the public – at least those who answer questionnaires – prefer 'spirituality' to religion. While you can read the same distinction into the Bible if you wish, it's not a native one. To put it in a more concrete way, the temple in Jerusalem was a model of the temple of the universe, and when the writer of Psalm 27 wants to "live always in God's house" and "enquire in his temple", he is saying that spirituality and religion are part of his whole life. Likewise, Qohelet, who might appear to the modern reader someone located in university rather than church, assumes in Chapter 5 that everyone will go to the house of God. But he adds, "To draw near to listen is better than the sacrifice of fools."

Then this Teacher reminds us rather cynically how economics and politics are tied together. Oppression and injustice are allowed to continue partly because of hierarchy: "My hands are tied by the system," says the lower down official in verse 8, or the person interviewing an asylum seeker. But at the same time, Qohelet says, you need some kind of system if the land is to prosper. Compared with a prophet like Amos, his politics are on the right. After warning us that money does not satisfy, he still ends the chapter by saying, "If God gives you wealth, enjoy it."

"But the next chapter contradicts all that," Jean pointed out. "The guy goes on to say that people get rich, but then it all goes to other people, even strangers."

"True," I said, "and he even says a still-born child may be happier – I think that is just another way of saying 'better never to be born' – and returns to saying all is vanity, just a puff of air. I'm not writing a poem on Chapter 6."

"You won't need to write one on Chapter 7 either," said Jean. "It's already a poem."

That was too much of a challenge. Qohelet's poem has a very disillusioned take on life, even fatalistic, where he says, "Consider the work of God; who can make straight what he has made crooked?" but at the same time he does go on to discuss life's riddles. Among these he rates woman, and blots his copybook for our generation by saying he finds one man in a thousand he can trust, but not one woman. John Goldingay in his practical commentary says this is a male leader giving his experience, so that women reading should simply turn it inside out and beware of men who may mislead them.[41] But finally Qohelet admits that we are all complex:

God made human beings straightforward,
but they have devised many schemes.

All in the Mind?

"God made us plain and simple,
but we have made ourselves very complicated" Ecclesiastes 7:29

I'm pulled, or pushed, this way and that
by currents somewhere in my mind.
Am I on course, or just on *khat*?[42]

Religion may be thought old hat,
while 'spirit' can be undefined.
I'm pulled, or pushed, this way or that.

Just who now seeks an automat
to wash their souls, and weekly find
they are on course, and not on *khat*?

I've had a life to get off pat
the words of faith, kind or unkind.
I'm pulled, or pushed, this way and that.

Whenever failure leaves me flat
the Devil puts me in a bind:
"Are you on course, or just on *khat*?"

There's no way off this wrestling mat
if faith is more than in the mind.
I'm pulled, or pushed, this way and that,
am I on course, or just on *khat*?

---

41 *Proverbs, Ecclesiastes and the Song of Songs for Everyone,* SPCK, London 2014, 207.

42 A drug chewed as a leaf in parts of Africa and Asia; Qohelet would probably have been familiar with it.

"I gave up the weekly religious automat in my teens," said Jean, "but I kept going to church occasionally, hoping to find something wise and kind which would make sense of life. Occasionally I did. Prayer didn't work for me, at least not the usual way. But I find some of your poems rather like a prayer."

"Thank you," I said, "they are to me. A poem of enquiry is really a prayer."

"I suppose by *khat* you are talking about living without thought, driven by the prevailing wind?"

"Yes. This can happen equally inside or out of the church, but I hope the prevailing wind inside is wiser and kinder."

Chapter 8 begins with a lovely word about wisdom, it "makes the face shine" – though some translations would just say it makes a man smile. But the chapter ends by admitting that however wise we are, we can't find out the meaning of what is going on. Before that, in the context of carrying out an order from the king which may be tricky, "The wise mind will know the time and the way". Here are three examples of those who subverted evil orders to save Jews in the early 1940s, from Poland, Lithuania and Hungary:

Saving Subversion

Oskar Schindler.   The orders were so serious,
he chewed on them, subverted them,
and listed Jews for Schindler's ark.

Chiune Sugihara.   He got his eggs from Tokyo,
preserved the shell and changed the yolk
into a visa for the refugees.

Raoul Wallenberg.   Chutzpah backed his fake *schutzpass*
which got them safe to Sweden,
lost the saviour in the *gulag*.

"What happened to that young Swedish diplomat?"

"Wallenberg was literally lost. He disappeared into the Soviet prison camp system, ignored by the Swedes and the Americans, last heard of in 1947 when his death was reported."

Qohelet wrote in Chapter 9 that a living dog is better than a dead lion. Lions don't give their lives for dogs in the animal kingdom (altruism would be confined to lions), but that kind of things does happen among humans. If the mystery of evil argues against God, the mystery of love and sacrifice is on the other side. Amidst the vagaries of time and chance, Qohelet simply says, life is short, so seize the day – "Whatever your hand finds to do, do it with all your might." Because death is coming, which ends all that.

Chapter 10 is a collection of observations, which you might sum up as saying, chance and folly can ruin anyone's life, but wisdom will sometimes help; and that any land is happier when it has a wise king. Some of the chapter is like Proverbs, for example the advice to watch what you say, even in your bedroom, for a little bird might tell tales.

A Little Bird Told Me

Watch the clever sparrow
hopping on the sill,
he's cocked a cunning ear or two
to catch some beans to spill.

Watch the long tailed tits
crowded in the tree,
sharing juicy worms of gossip
straight from you and me.

Watch the dapper goldfinch,
perched there on his own,
beneath that flashy feather coat
he hides a microphone.

Watch the yellowhammer's
wee encyclopaedia;
he has your details written down
and trolls on social media.

"It was an excuse for a poem for children," I told Jean.

"There is one reference in Ecclesiastes to young people, but you're a chapter ahead," she replied. You need a poem on foreign trade for Chapter 11, first."

The point Qohelet makes is really about spreading your investments, though in the context of trading abroad. The risk is mainly storms at sea, but the advice is definitely to take the risk (rather than always fearing the weather), and let the ships sail.

Let the Ships Sail

China's all around me,
cautiously in the Economist,
commonly upon the internet,
gung-ho from Ambassador Liu,
interviewed by Andrew Marr, probing
claims of genocide.

Huawei's all around me,
somewhere deep within my broadband use,
ship of fortune with the trade winds changed,
relic of enthusiastic deals, now sin-binned,
banned and due for breaking up:
Britain follows USA.

Fears may be justified,
or not, and yes, a trade war must be better
than the other kind. I heard him cite
a Chinese emperor, who had no need
for trade. This caused a century's decline,
he said: Britain beware!

Before the short epilogue, Ecclesiastes has a memorable section on youth and age. As a poetic account of old age, Ecclesiastes 12 has never been bettered. At the close, our dust (body) returns to the earth, and our breath (spirit) to God.

"What do you think of that as a statement of what happens at the end?" asked Jean.

"It's as simple and profound as ever. And strangely modern. It's popular to say that we are made of stardust, and clearly our bodies rot in the ground."

"So why are Christians so leery of admitting that the bones of Jesus rotted away too?"

"Because we find the historical evidence for the empty tomb compelling."[43]

Jean and I could have spent a long time on this, but we agreed that it would be better to leave it to a future book on the four Gospels. Like most of the Old Testament, Qohelet did not believe in resurrection, though by the time of Jesus, there were a variety of views. Sadducees (the conservatives) held to the view there was no resurrection. Some held the Greek view that the body perished, but the soul lived on. The Pharisees (radicals in this at least) believed that we died, and would be in the end resurrected.[44] 'Resurrection' could be applied to the nation, to individual bodies, or both.

Daniel 12 was one passage which supported that view – there, Daniel is promised that along with the righteous he will rise again "at the end of the days". Now, Daniel is present at the notorious Belshazzar's feast, where a mysterious hand writes judgment on the wall, and the same night the Babylonian empire falls. According to Qohelet – a very different kind of statesman from Daniel – a land is happy when its princes feast at the proper time (Ecclesiastes 10:17), but Belshazzar's time was up, as in this poem on the book of Daniel:

---

43 This is thoroughly researched (more than 700 pages!) in N T. Wright, *The Resurrection of the Son of God*, SPCK, London 2003.

44 There are different views in the apocryphal writings: 2 Maccabees believes in bodily resurrection, 4 Maccabees has gone back to immortality of the soul.

Dreams and Disability

In her dreams, a girl in a wheelchair is walking;
four captives in Babylon are baulking
at the crush of exile; they push
against obesity of soul and body,
thin out their options, study,
graduate in faith and culture.

In his dreams, a king in a palace is fabled,
then cut down to size, disabled,
driven out of office and society.
Listen: disability has no respect
for race or face, or power of place.
You dream of who you really are.

In its cups, an elite at a banquet is scared
by God's own verdict, unprepared
for what lies round the corner.
Every crash is obvious in hindsight,
foresight needs the dreaming prophet,
and the team of Daniel and Darius.

In the epilogue at the close, Qohelet – or the writer who has used
him to put forward a range of views – returns to the orthodox
belief that we should "fear God and keep his commandments".
Before than, typically, he gives us two (different) 'last words' on
wisdom:

(a) The sayings of the wise are 'goads', they stimulate us.

(b) No end to the books being published – study just tires
you out.

Book Festival

The old converse, the young have given up
their latest mobiles for the laughing gas
which giggles cheerfully around the square,
digs over-serious in their solemn ribs,
finds a way to infiltrate the speech
of poets, journos, writers, politicians
– all this expert chunter needing air
to light or lighten up their flow of words,
ignite a spiel of intimacy, touching
table talk for those and such as those
who like to eat and drink celebrity.

The sayings of the wise are pointed sticks
which poke some rockets into politics;
but end to end these titles only reach
from Charlotte Square to Portobello Beach.

"I am a rose of Sharon, a lily of the valleys." Song of Songs 2:1

Chapter 6   Song of Songs

"I'm still thinking about Porty beach," said Jean. "I used to go there sometimes with Harry. He had a flat in Portobello."

Jean had once mentioned Harry to me, but I had never felt I should ask about him. This time I felt the door was open. "Tell me about Harry," I asked. She did. Harry was the only man she had ever been really close to. He was a widower, the father of a girl in her sixth form. She had got to know him, and after the girl had left school she had begun visiting his flat. They were, as Jean put it rather quaintly to me, an item – I didn't ask what form the relationship took. But from her eyes and voice I knew she must have fallen deeply in love. It was a good start to our conversation about the Song of Songs, which can mean either "the best song" or "one of a collection of songs".

The poem begins with a concatenation of sibilants: the title of the Song is in Hebrew *shir-ha-shirim*, and it begins with *yishakeni minshikot* (let him kiss me with kisses); and later we have *shoshana* (lily), and the girl herself is the Shulamite.

Sister Sibilants

Every language has its style,
in English it's like this:
just let your cheeks' smile squish
a shh into a sss,
switch pet to crocodile,
sweet kiss to squash and cuss,
in one swish, hiss or diss.

Unlike Ecclesiastes, and unlike that poem, there is not a touch of cynicism in the Song. Rabbi Akiva said that the Song of Songs was the Holy of Holies (*kodesh kodashim*).

"That's a rather odd thing to say," said Jean, whose RE lessons had obviously steered clear of this book.

"It is. But he was in tune with the early Church Father Origen, even though Origen was single and the rabbi was married; and although Origen was so tormented by his sexuality that he went and got himself castrated, Akiva was deeply in love with his wife Rachel."

"As I read it, it's just a love song, or maybe a collection of poems that have got put together."

"The rabbi and the theologian both saw it as an allegory all through. For example, when the Song refers to the beloved as 'a dove in the clefts of the rock', for Origen the dove emerges from the rock of Christ, while for Akiva the dove emerges from the rocks of Sinai. Other Jewish commentators see the Song as being all about the crossing of the Red Sea, and the mystical Zohar takes the Song as being about everything in the universe!"[45]

Veiled Meaning

Love wears a veil,
there is a time and place to lift it,
pin it back with faithfulness and passion.

Life wears a veil,
until we grasp it in the poetry
and prose of someone really gracious.

God wears a veil,
but gives us words to lift it,
lift us into ecstasy of union.

---

45 Ilana Pardes goes into all this in detail in her book *The Song of Songs: A Biography*, Princeton University Press, Princeton NJ 2019.

For the medieval monk Bernard of Clairvaux, the Song was about the soul and the love of Christ for us. Because of his desire for that ecstasy of union with the divine, he preached 86 sermons on the book with hardly a step beyond Chapters 1 and 2. And there were later enthusiasts like Teresa of Avila who spoke of the Christian life as beginning with kissing the feet of the divine Lover, then progressing to kissing the hand, and for a few reaching the stage of kissing his mouth. John of the Cross wrote a commentary on the book while he was imprisoned in a cell only ten feet by six. They all saw the Song as an allegory.

Jean was a bit sceptical. "Why didn't they see it for what it is, a simple love song?"

"It was because they did see it that way that they could see beyond it as well. For every person like Origen who was embarrassed by their sexuality, there was another who saw sexuality as sacramental. I think that is why the Song has attracted so many people from different backgrounds, even though we know perfectly well that the poems are not that different from, say, Syrian wedding songs."

Sexuality

Cracking open of the crooked heart.
Turning Freud the right way up.
Spirit of God in the secret place.
Spark of God, waiting for a match.
The mystery under the *chuppah*,
shawl to shield and sanctify the pair.
Sex and sanctuary, sanctuary and sex.[46]

I was struck by this sense of sanctuary in a foreign culture, travelling, as it happened, on the number 7 bus in Edinburgh:

---

46 One or two thoughts in this poem I owe to Sarah Coakley, *God, Sexuality and the Self*, Cambridge University Press, Cambridge 2013, 24.

Culture Clash

She was black and beautiful,
hair locked and braided, fourth
finger ringed and signalling
a greater cult than 'me',
with a full year's worth of
baby locked into a pram.
Ironic, that such iconic
keys to happiness should be
well oiled in other cultures,
but so fusty, rusty here, interred
in western fear that wedlock
equals hemlock; so we tug
our disappearing forelocks
to the myth that love can only
flourish in a universe parallel
to one with old lovelock and key.

"The Victorians had their share of hypocrisy," said Jean, "but they did realise that sex is spoiled when it is too much in the open."

"Like those old Hitchcock films, which always just hinted at the horror; they were far more powerful than the modern throw-it-in-your-face genre."

"I can see that the Song of Songs gets it right – it has no qualms about talking breasts and thighs, but it leaves the fulfilment beyond the poem."

"And one thing is very topical – 1:5, where the girl says outright, 'I am black and beautiful'. Great slogan for 'Black Lives Matter' today. Though last century, when 'Black is Beautiful' was a campaign slogan, I don't remember the Song getting any credit."

Black and Beautiful

A colour to dance upon prejudice,
stamp on a passport to pride,
clasp in the strong, safe muscles
of conviction that the human brush
is painting some respect
on the world's white canvas.

In the song itself, the girl is probably comparing herself not to people we brand 'white' today, but to lighter skinned city women. Her skin has been darkened by manual work outside (1:6), so there is not only a blow against racial but against class prejudice: love tears off these labels. While older people often ask whether such border crossings will stand the test of time, the Song's one venture into 'wisdom' is the refrain, addressed to the daughters of Jerusalem: "Do not stir up or awaken love until it is ready!"

I see no difficulty in taking this love song as about both human love and divine love. This is certainly the Jewish tradition, and Christians are used to thinking God and human together because of what they believe about Jesus Christ. There is one inversion in the Song which may or may not be deliberate, but it casts light on the journey of both kinds of love:

2:16   My beloved is mine, and I am his
6:3   I am my beloved's, and my beloved is mine

When we first fall in love, with God or with another person, we are typically engrossed with what it means for us, how wonderful it feels to 'possess' the other. But as we mature, as our love grows deeper, we begin more and more to put the other first.

I was discussing this with Jean, when she broke in: "I was deeply in love with Harry. He was English, but that didn't matter. His grandfather came from India, but that didn't matter. He was a Christian, and because I was in love, I went to church with him. And then . . . and then they diagnosed his cancer. He only lived a few months more. I had tasted something wonderful, and it was snatched away."

"Does that make it really hard looking at this book?"

"Yes and no. It was years ago, and I have learned to live without it. You could say I have an idea what heaven is like, if it exists."

Zoom is not the easiest medium for this level of conversation. I asked Jean if she'd like a break, but she told me she wanted to say something about the Song of Songs. "This book seems like a dream sequence. Sometimes the lover seems to be Solomon, sometimes a young shepherd boy; there is a dream in Chapter 3, a nightmare in Chapter 5; in the last chapter the girl seems to come home. The verse which sums this up for me is 5:2, 'I slept, but my heart was awake'. Is love, is the love of God, a kind of dream? For believers, is death a rude awakening, or nothing, or some kind of fulfilment?"

"Jean, as you know only too well, I can't prove to you or anyone that God is real. When a believer feels the love of God, she doesn't say God is there because she feels that way, or even because she thinks that way, but because God is Spirit; the Spirit knows what is going on inside us and delights to be part of that."

"When Harry was alive, I knew that love was real, and I thought that God was real too. But when I lost Harry, I lost God also."

I knew the best thing I could do was just listen. In the end I did say I would try to write a poem about dreams, reality, and the Song of Songs. A tall order. It's never easy writing a poem for someone, especially when loss is part of it. I based it on 5:2-8.

Jean's Dream

I wore him, wondering – smock and sari,
sweat and silk – I wore him, body and soul;
but now he sleeps, a million miles away,
heart closed to me, and to the world he'd known,
his body burned, his soul – well, what is that?
I tried to hold it fast somewhere inside me,
but it proved as empty as my own.

I have taken off my love clothes now,
there is a time for this, a time for that.
One corner of my heart could hear a knock,
repeated twice; the rest just gave a yawn;
I dreamed of God, his hand upon the latch,
and in my dream I woke and said "I'm here,"
like Samuel, but of course I found he'd gone.

I soon learned to make something to wear,
covered soul and body with intelligence
– of what, I sometimes ask myself.
Yes, I fear the thought police may even
steal my home made clothes and batter me;
but I have tasted love, and have to muse
if any of my gowns were made in heaven.

I suppose I was taking a liberty with the start of the poem, as it might have seemed intrusive, but Jean said she was deeply touched by the poem. We closed the session, and agreed to look at the identity of the characters next time.

Solomon is named as the author of the Song, but that could be understood in many ways. The rabbis took him as the author, but at the same time insisted that he was speaking allegorically of events like the Exodus long before his time. 1 Kings 4:32 tells us that Solomon composed over a thousand songs, but many of the expressions in the poem are as late as the Persian period, so modern scholarship has generally assumed that different poems have been brilliantly combined into a sequence which allows different interpretations. The beloved is clearly the Shulamite maiden, whoever she is, but the identity of the lover ranges from Solomon as shepherd-king to a simple shepherd whose beloved is rescued from the arrogant clutches of Solomon, with of course the Lord God as the divine lover behind the scenes.

The Shulamite

Naebodie kens yer faither.
Yer aw yersel, wumman
– nae strind, nae kin,   *lineage family*
jist a birlin, whurlin body   *person*
sookin up the warld lik a magnet.
Wha wadna loo ye,   *love*
lang tae woo ye, hap ye   *wrap*
in is airms, pree yer mou,   *kiss*
gang a the wey wi ye,
lukin in yer een fur a thoosan years?   *eyes*
Abody spiers aboot ye,   *asks*
gaes oan aboot ye, mervels
hoo ye cam by sic lik smeddum.   *such spirited character*
Bit A'm by spierin, fearin: *past asking*
jist dookin ma heid richt unner yer spell.

"Why did you write that poem in Scots?" asked Jean.

Why indeed? When you inhabit a different culture you become a different person. Maybe I write in Scots because I enjoy that freedom. But I gave Jean a mundane reason.

"I think it was because she seemed just a local lassie. The great thing about the Song is that at one level it is a love poem about ordinary people, and then at the deeper level it tells us that God's love is also for ordinary people, and perhaps especially for those who find themselves on their own, like the Shulamite."

Or you, Jean, I thought. Without your Solomon. In this chapter the lover has become a royal, who invites his bride to ride beside him in a chariot. Yet a likely translation of 6:12 is that "my *fancy* set me in a chariot beside my prince". Is it all imagination? Or is it simply that the magic of love turns a shepherd into a prince? The Song offers us all these interpretations in the rich experience of love.

As far as love is concerned, royalty is usually more convincing in the imagination than in reality. In 1995, Princess Diana felt so isolated, with her marriage irretrievably broken down, that she sought a BBC Panorama interview in order to give her side of the story.

Diana

She took a shattered fairy tale
and gave the pieces to the likes of us
who blessed her honesty, and felt her pain,
and built a palace for her service.

Chapter 7 is very good for straight-nosed Westerners to read, because it asserts the beauty of the bigger nose characteristic of Middle Eastern people (7:4). Bible versions generally divide up the text between three parties, the lover, the Shulamite and the bystanders (the women of Jerusalem), so that in Chapter 7 it is obvious that the lover praises the girl up to verse 9, and then the girl invites her lover to consummate the relationship.

Chapter 8 then begins rather oddly to our ears, with a wish that the lover was a brother – but the point seems to be merely that this would allow the lovers to be together without the critical comments which clearly the girl fears.

The chorus "Do not awaken love until it is ready" at 8:4 is a natural conclusion to the book, but instead we have a selection of individual verses, some of which are closer to wisdom teaching, like "Many waters cannot quench love". Then for only the second time in the book we have what some might call a male authority figure. In 5:7 we had the watchman assaulting the girl in the streets, and now in 8:8-9 the brothers say how they will protect a girl before puberty – as older male figures might well do in any culture, of course. But there may be a hint that the girl has been in danger of being treated as 'property' to be bargained with, so from verse 10 the girl takes over the story; back in 4:12 the lover says that she is "a garden locked"; but now she has opened her garden to her Solomon.

Different commentaries tell the story in different ways, and bring out a variety of motifs. One is the reference to "coming up from the wilderness" (or desert); first in 3:6, where Solomon is being carried in state, and then in 8:5 when the girl is "leaning on her beloved". Robert Fyall suggests that "the great romance of God with his people" (bringing them out of slavery in Egypt) is repeated in this love story of a girl and a boy,[47] or a woman and Solomon. This of course is why the rabbis saw the Song as an allegory of the Exodus.

A big idea: it warranted a final poem, but I couldn't get what Jean had told me out of my mind, and I decided I would write another poem for her. That was dangerous enough, but as I thought about the Song, I realised it had to be a *ghazal*, a Middle East love poem, put into the mouth of Harry. There are strict rules for this kind of poem, but as with the sonnet, contemporary poets relax them; I have however, kept many of the rules – as an outsider, I must respect these beautiful things. Those who dislike the allegorical meaning of the Song can simply leave out the opening and closing stanzas.

---

47 Fyall 2005, 148.

Flowers

It took them all their time to cross the desert,
treading on the sand, and hidden flowers.

It was a late awakening to a dream
that touched on true, for it was truly ours.

Five years had held me in their lonely grasp
and squeezed me dry, like wilted desert flowers.

Four drops of rain woke up the waiting seeds,
and grew my love among the desert flowers.

It was a late awakening to a dream
that touched on true, for it was truly ours.

Three words we spoke before our pupils met
and drew our hands to touch behind the flowers.

Two blossoms lie within my heart, the crocus[48]
and the lily, raw rare desert flowers.

It was a late awakening to a dream
that touched on true, for it was truly ours.

One month of pain, but greater loss to know
my love is left to wait, like desert flowers.

It takes God all his time to keep on watch
for love to grow, and nourish hidden flowers.

---

48 A more likely translation than the "rose" of Sharon (2:1).

"The Lord has become like an enemy . . . he has destroyed all its palaces, laid in ruins all its strongholds."   Lamentations 2:5

Chapter 7 Lamentations

From a love poem to Lamentations seems a leap into despair, incongruous for the comfortably off, but not before time for those on the underside of conflict, ill health and injustice.

At the end of the last poem, God was "staying on watch" for love to grow. But what kind of watch? A God watching as a farmer watches a growing crop? Willing to help, if asked? Or watching sadly or even cynically, as things fall apart? Here is how I imagine the people of Lewis after *The Iolaire* tragedy:

Our Dust

You turn us back to dust, dust blown
off course, unable to make landfall,
ravaged by rocks, the desert sea, and worse,
grounded by our past, our wilderness,
our memory of Moses silent,
our memory of David gone so sour.

Our dust the Iolaire Inquiry gathered
in official vaults for fifty years,
while we had lost the wounded words,
pulled our fingers from the chanter,
placed our fiddles in the closet
where a silent tide washed over them.

A hundred years have nursed this silence,
grown the roots of trauma underground,
with our fury burned up in the psalms,
our sadness shivering on the sands
of Stornoway and every sermon
hinting at some sin still stowed away.

Theology – God-talk – is a risky business. Qohelet said (Ecclesiastes 5:2), "Let your words be few." Indeed there is a tradition of silence, as well as the *via negativa* of saying "God is not this, not that . . ." Yet the Old Testament is not silent about God. What it does, however, is give us a number of different languages – narrative, novel, proverb, poetry, praise . . . and now lament.

This teaches that the God who reveals himself in word is yet beyond these words, so that we need words used in different ways if we are not only to cope with life in all its aspects but find God in all of them. And a world where tragedy can strike anywhere and everywhere needs lament. But what is striking, even shocking about this book of Lamentations is that God is no longer on the sidelines, watching with sympathy. Rather, God has become the enemy who has brought disaster on his people, grinding their faces in the dust.

Which takes us to the first poem. The form of a sestina is designed to build up a picture by repeating words in different contexts, which gradually increases the feeling that nothing is holding things together except a few words, and ends by rubbing the reader's nose in those six words.

Lost Civilisation

A litany of death connects the world,
disaster joins the poetry of then and now;
and while we gag and find tears prick
our eyes, the fire keeps running,
overtaking people, history and culture,
burning like the anger of a god.

"That's it!" some cry, "The vengeance of a God
ignored and slighted: all across the world
it's blasphemy and pornographic culture
that is thriving, driving our affairs. Now
listen to the revelation; hear the running
feet, feel the terror and the sword prick!"

"Primitive! Our god is education. Prick
that ancient bubble of belief in God.
Learn from westerners just how to run
a modern democratic state; world
affairs are our responsibility. Now
you have the chance, renew your culture!"

So the bombs and bullets fly. A culture
dies, heads roll, and no-one's prick
or pussy's torture-proof, for now
the ancient laws are gone; that god
indeed is dead, and all the world
is mad; marauders make the running.

Tragedy and tears just keep on running
as two enemies collude to make a culture
bloody hell. Just what in all the world
will change the grisly game, and prick
the conscience of the blind, find a God
of mercy, halt the slaughter here and now?

The Middle East's a cockpit, then and now.
It shows us human sin and sorrow, running
through its history, and bumping into God
who wears them, bears them in the culture
of a seed that grew to let God prick
out bold a seedling hope for all the world.

Lament is there to prick the tumours
of the world's despair, to hold a culture
running out of time. Now, where is God?

The word rotation of a sestina introduces an element of craziness – there is a pattern, but it doesn't really make sense of what is being said. Rather like Lamentations itself: the first chapter is written by someone who knows exactly why disaster has happened, and has chosen a tight alphabetical pattern, with each verse starting with a different letter of the Hebrew alphabet; but by the end of the book, disaster is the dreadful same, but now beyond reason and beyond hope. Running out of time indeed, as we fail miserably either to act together on climate change, or stop the wars that crop up in places we have forgotten about. And yet the book is carefully crafted, with each chapter either 22 verses (the number of letters in the alphabet), or a multiple of that.

"I see what you mean," said Jean, who had been reading a commentary on Lamentations.[49] "A tight structure which gradually loosens, until the last chapter is just an echo, holding on to its 22 verses, but no structure beyond that. But your structure is the other way round, it builds until the last triplet forces all the words together."

"True. Yet having held on to something about God all through, I end up with God's absence. And although I seem to confidently state things about God, in fact God never speaks – in the poem, or in Lamentations."

"That seems to have been true most of the way through all these books we have looked at. In Ruth God is assumed in the story, in Esther God is not mentioned at all, in Job God only enters right at the end, in Proverbs God is referred to in just a few of the sayings; Ecclesiastes takes a pretty cynical view of God, in the Song of Songs God disappears again, and now we have Lamentations. We didn't need God to enjoy the love poetry, and after Lamentations is there any point at all in religion?"

---

49 Kathleen O'Connor, *Lamentations and the Tears of the World*, Orbis, Maryknoll NY 2002.

What I wanted to say was that the decision to include such a book in the canon of Scripture was a sign that lament might be a gift to the real tragic world we lived in, but something in Jean's tone of voice was telling me this was getting personal. So I changed tack.

"Jean," I said. "In poetry love and loss are often woven together. I was trying to do that in the poem I wrote for you."

"Thank you. But I don't feel there are any flowers left for God to nourish, hidden or not. And it's not just my loss of faith. It's gone from our culture, from Scotland, from Britain. When the pandemic began, BBC1 television re-introduced a Sunday morning service as well as Songs of Praise. It didn't last, just like the way people have tired of their initial public courtesy in the street. In fact, Europe has quietly thrown away her Christian moorings, apart from Hungary, but there it seems a political thing. America seems to have made faith a commodity for aspiring public figures to buy. It may be around somewhere in Asia and Africa and South America, but here it has disappeared from public life."

I told Jean that our conversation seemed to me a good way of approaching the book, and we agreed to look at it more closely. I was aware that Lamentations spoke directly to situations like the Holocaust, and to issues like the legacy of black slavery, but that the loss Jean was talking about was something gentler, more of a disappearance than a disaster. The dissolution of public religion, which had happened slowly over the past fifty years, and its replacement by a smorgasbord of private beliefs and practices. The disappearance of public truth, even sometimes where science was concerned, and the growth of habits of suspicion which have replaced trust.

Lamentations is already great poetry, but I said I would try something, make it short, and do my best to catch this sense of disappearance.

Lost

The well is dry.
A few tourists
scan the grille,
tell their friends
'There is mud
at the bottom'.

The house is sad.
She still talks
to her man
in soft whispers,
remembers all
the bustle of life.

The net is busy
catching videos,
blogs, posts, likes.
Through the holes,
truth swims away
without connection.

"That's certainly a lot more gentle than Lamentations. I read there how God sent fire into the bones of Jerusalem, and ground the teeth of its people into the gravel!"

"The description of suffering would be familiar to anyone who endured siege or genocide – Leningrad, Darfur, Aleppo, places like that."

"But what jars on me is the idea that God was responsible!"

"It's not generally how we do theology today. It was part of the calvinist tradition which poets like Iain Crichton Smith experienced and hated. But there are three things about it which I want to hold onto. First, that God has freely chosen to make the world as it is, full of risks; therefore, God is to a degree responsible for all that goes on, which means that at least we have someone to hurl our questions at. Second, that we share a common human responsibility for the world's troubles, so we need to own up to our sin and do something about it. Third – and maybe this joins the first two together – that God holds us accountable as our judge. What softens the calvinist view is that God judges his people in order to save them, and that God is actually with his people in their suffering – though in Scripture these notes are sounded at different times, whereas theology tries to think them together."

"Well, Lamentations has plenty of confession! But also the desolation of not being able to anything about it. The pandemic showed us that we could easily rejig our economic system to help the poor and save the planet, if we wanted to – but the world is full of people who can do little or nothing about their fate."

"And many of us in the West feel that way too. Truth swims away, the house is sad, the well is dry."

"You said God is our judge," insisted Jean. "But how does that work in an age when people ignore him? We make our own judgments about our leaders, even if we can't change much."

"Remember I quoted C.S. Lewis: 'God whispers to us in our happiness and shouts to us in our pain'?"

"So the pandemic was a judgment?"

"I would say more of a judgment call. God obviously allows it, and (like everything else) he uses it. God is calling out the consequences of human behaviour, and calling on us to make our situation an opportunity for repentance, for a change that might save the situation. But there are at least two more things to be said about judgment. One of them comes in Chapter 3, at the centre of the book – and in Middle Eastern story-telling, that is often where the climax comes."[50]

---

50 Kenneth Bailey, *Poet and Peasant*, Eerdmans, Grand Rapids 1976, 50.

Great is Thy Faithfulness[51]

What a hymn to snatch from Lamentations,
leaving most of it a scream of protest.
God's own hand did built a wall about them,
sure, but just to shackle them, the target
for his arrows shot at skeleton flesh.
Morning by morning they gasped and they cried,
season by season they shuddered and died.

Witness chokes us with the dreadful shadow
of a God whose judgment never changes,
every vein of hope a mirage. Women
boil their children, hopeless cannibals,
their human nature crushed and torn to shreds.
Morning by morning new terrors they saw,
season by season their wounds bled them raw.

What a hymn, chiselled by Thomas Chisholm
out of stony horror, choosing rather
resurrection on the third of days,
chapter three of life and death and what
comes next, a confidence not in the text.
Morning by morning new mercies I see,
season by season, a skeleton key.

"You seem determined to make some sense of the tragedy," said Jean.

"There is a time to lament, Ecclesiastes told us, but then we resume our incurable urge to make sense of the universe. One Bible version follows that great poem about a time for this and that with the recognition that 'God has put eternity into our hearts'.[52]

---

51   I owe the unusual angle on a famous and much loved hymn to a conversation with David Smith (see his book, *Stumbling Towards Zion*, Langholm Global Library, Carlisle 2020).

52   Ecclesiastes 3:11.

The different between belief and unbelief is that the believer thinks she is responding to a sense already there, the atheist that all this is 'mere poetry'; the word 'mere' downgrades poetry to being nothing more than our best words."

"Are words all we have?" asked Jean. "Some of the time," I replied, "but there is always more, whether it comes through the words or quite unexpectedly."

Faith

> The devil's a good theologian, though
> he likes to give such words a twist;
> 'good' is unfortunately lost in the mist
> of 'faith is what I believe'. And so,
> we'll give it a whirl, hope for the best,
> look on the bright side, chin up to the breeze,
> keep in with the crowd, believe what we please
> and hope it will never be put to the test.
> But what about Faith with a capital F?
> Well, such a creed is a series of words,
> and the word on the street says it's only for nerds
> such as bikers and bishops, the odd holy chef
> who will cook up a reason or two to believe.
> Disappointed? Just stay around, on the *qui vive*!

On reflection, I had two further thoughts. First, there are some things we should simply oppose rather than try to make sense of. Evil is one of them. If someone is gunning for you, while an explanation may help, a line of defence (or even attack) may be the first thing needed. Jesus argued with people, but simply commanded evil spirits. Second, in many circumstances we do well simply to plant something new in the midst of the old, and let it grow – whether that be a kind act, a loving presence, or a wise story. Jesus said the kingdom of God was like a grain of mustard seed; and as the new grows up it will replace the old more effectively than argument or opposition.

When I mentioned all this to Jean she was not impressed. "You are back in your armchair," she said, "enjoying the luxury of digression. That's exactly what Job's friends did – they trotted out all their wisdom to Job, instead of listening to where he was coming from. The people of Jerusalem who survived the massacre were starving, they didn't have any seed to plant, they didn't have the energy to do anything. You'd better feel the pain and write a poem about that!"

We had reached Chapters 3 and 4. I thought of the Psalms of Asaph in the third book of the Old Testament Psalms, which reflect that awful period in Israel's history. There is a word in several of the psalms, *selah*; it comes at intervals, and no one really knows what it means. That seems to fit the desolation of Lamentations, and the desolation of Middle East refugees today.

Selah

Zabiullah sips tea in a tent;
stench of sewage hangs around
him and seven thousand others,
waiting for news of asylum,
watching a rat scuttle past.[53]
Selah.

"This is worse than the boat,"
he says, caught in an eternity
hung around his neck:
queueing for toilets, ten minutes,
queueing for bread, ten hours,
queueing for asylum, ten months.
Selah.

---

53 This is based on a story in *The Economist*, 3 Nov. 2018, 'A Small Piece of Hell', 34.

Lesbos, island of loitering,
loitering in tent and trauma,
loitering in mental breakdown,
loitering under the leaky umbrella
of that deal with Turkey,
put up fast to block
the heavy rain of refugees.
Selah.

"We are treated worse than animals,"
Somali teen Saida says,
fighting months of boredom,
fighting for a doctor,
struggling for identity
against the lure of suicide.
Selah.

God has set a time, *Selah*,
to judge with equity, *Selah*.
Selah – silent pause
which echoes all our questions,
leaves us none the wiser.
Selah.

"I hear an echo when I read Lamentations," said Jean. "The lament of those from the awful Syrian civil war in places like Homs and Aleppo. Indeed, everyone who's lost their home in the Middle East."

"If that is really an echo," I said, "then a terrible judgment may fall on the western powers who ousted Saddam Hussein with shock and awe and then left the Middle East to its fate. I say that because of how the prophets saw Babylon: God's instrument of judgment on Israel, yes, but because they overstepped the mark they would be judged in turn. Just like Israel's sister nation Edom." (4:21-22)

"That sounds too much like fatalism to me. I don't think events are predictable like that."

"There may be a safer model in 4:20, which talks about the Lord's anointed, 'the breath of their life.'"

"Presumably King Zedekiah – according to Jeremiah a bad king who broke his promise to the Babylonians, and brought disaster on Israel."

"But also a way of talking about the Messiah that Israel came to expect. Makes me think of Jews in exile living under the shadow of God's promise, 'among the nations'. Christians likewise, as we name Jesus 'Christ', which means the anointed one."

Beyond Measure

Preachers chasten us with messages of doom:
we have forgotten God, we must clean up
the cobwebs of our dirty minds, spend time
in prayer, be firmer in our faith. Then God
will bless us, strengthen sinews in the State,
and all our preachers will be duly grateful,
better paid, things as they should be.

Lamentations is no place for easy preachers,
nor a field to pick bright illustrations,
flowers to wear in happy buttonholes.
Switch the sermon: God may have forgotten
people, preacher, skirt and sanctuary,
gone walkabout from mind and memory, closed
the book on faith, on hope, on everything.

How can we measure God for any suit or skirt,
divine intention put inside a fitting room
to make God fit our image, box him into shape
and keep his thoughts and feelings for us safe?
If we are so sure God's anger grinds us
into dust, is it just possible his mercy
might be there as well, to raise the dust?

One of the reassuring things about the Bible is that while there is an overall message of hope, it allows things that seem to contradict each other to jostle within it, such as the message of hope at the end of Chapter 4 – God will keep Israel in exile no longer – and the prayer out of misery in Chapter 5, which ends with the awful possibility that things have gone too far, that God has utterly rejected his people.

I say reassuring for at least two reasons: first, that those who edited the Bible did not try to 'fix' the writings which they included in the canon of holy scripture, and second, because these different messages make sense of the contradictions of life today. Different people need different verses at different times.

"I think I've always recognised that," said Jean. "What I find hard, is to trust that overall message of hope. Harry did, I once thought I did, but it died with him."

"And your brother?"

"Yes, he had a strong faith. But for him it was a rescue out of brokenness. My life has always been respectable."

"Have any of these seven books really spoken to you?

"Hm . . . Ruth and Esther are great stories, and Job is a classic. Plenty of wisdom in Proverbs and Ecclesiastes. The Song of Songs was beautiful, and but also quite painful, though I have this hope – or is it delusion? – that the experience of love really is a kind of intimation of something greater and more lasting. Then Lamentations: Lamentations is the kind of book that should sink all hope without trace, but it didn't have that effect on me. In the troubled world we live in, we need it. And those pinpricks of light – 'The Lord is good to those who wait for him' is a verse I think I may hang on to, even if I'm still not sure that there is a God there at all."

And that was where we left it. Only I found myself turning Jean's last thought the other way round. The picture that came to me was of a God who is more real than we are, patiently feeding a shadowy person who is beginning to take shape. Which I thought might be true of both Jean and myself.

"The sayings of the wise are like goads, and like nails firmly fixed are
the collected sayings that are given by one shepherd."
Ecclesiastes 12:11

Index of Names, Places and Topics

K

Khayyam, Omar 69
Kipling, Rudyard 31

L

lament 95–108
Lamentations 6, 95–108
law 10
Leningrad, seige of 100
Leonardo da Vinci 18
Lesbos 105
Levenson, J.D. 71
Lewis, C.S. 16, 47, 58–59, 101
Lithuania 76
loss 52, 99–100
love 2, 5–7, 83–94, 99, 107

M

MacIntyre, Alasdair 23
Mao Zedong 55
Marcion 10–11
Marr, Andrew 78
marriage 10–11, 17, 19 20, 62–63, 85
Mary, mother of Jesus 62
Matthew 2–3
McGilchrist, Iain 71
McGrath, Alister 23
McLeish, Tom 29, 41
Mehanovic, Samir 25
Messiah 1, 3, 106
Miller, Mary 14
Moabites iii, 2
Mordecai 14–28
Moses 4, 60, 95
Mulder, Karen 41

N

Naomi 2–12

Nehemiah 14
Newman, Cardinal 22–23
Norgrove, Linda 17
North Korea 13

O

Obed viii, 4, 9
O'Connor, Kathleen 98
Oliver, Neil 11
Origen 84

P

Pardes, Ilana 84
Peck, John 41–43
Peterson, Eugene 9, 68
philosophy 1, 39, 41, 51, 70
Pinsky, Rob 69
poetry 49
  appreciation of iv, 29
  forms of 1, 33, 35, 62, 66, 72, 75, 92, 96
Poland 76
politics 8, 11, 74, 76, 99
Porteous, Norman 47
Portobello 81, 83
Port Seton 60–61
prayer 19, 45, 51, 58, 76
predestination 31
pride 23–25, 56, 67
Provan, Iain 7
Proverbs 8, 19, 47–64, 98, 107
providence 5, 14–15, 23–25, 50
Psalms 104
Puah 19
Purim, festival of 14, 21

Q

Qohelet 65–82, 96
quantum physics 22, 55

Index of Books, Plays and Poems

*Author's Poems in bold
Books and Plays in italics*

Index of Scripture References

Other books by the author are available in the Handsel Press bookstore (google 'Handsel Press Store'):

https://buy.sanctusmedia.com/store/collections/handsel-press-store